FASAB's STRATEGIC DIRECTIONS

Federal Accounting Standards Advisory Board

Clarifying FASAB's Near-Term Role in Achieving the Objectives of Federal Financial Reporting

November 2006

Table of Contents

Abbreviations i

Executive Summary ii

Introduction and Scope 1

Introduction and Scope 2

    Objectives Phase of the Concepts Project - Evaluate Objectives 2

SFFAC 1 Status 3

Defining FASAB's Strategic Directions by Clarifying the Board's Near-Term Role in
Achieving the Broad Objectives of Financial Reporting 5

    Consideration of the Mission of FASAB 5

    Consideration of the Current Language in Concepts Statements 6

    Consideration of the Comparative Advantages as a GAAP Standard-Setter 8

    Consideration of the Evolution of Federal Financial Management and New Laws and
    Administrative Directives 10

    Consideration of the Results from Roundtable Meetings on each Objective 12

    Consideration of Other Factors such as Other Reports Fulfilling the Objectives and
    the Contribution of Current Standards 13

Assessment of FASAB's Near-Term Role in Achieving Each Objective 15

FASAB's Primary Near-Term Focus Objectives 16

FASAB's Secondary Near-Term Focus Objectives 26

Conclusion on FASAB's Strategic Directions 36

APPENDIX I – Criteria for Ranking Projects 37

APPENDIX II--Evolution in FASAB 38

APPENDIX III--GAAP AND NON-GAAP REPORTING 43

APPENDIX IV--Evolution in Federal Financial Management and Reporting Laws and
Administrative Directives since the CFO Act of 1990 46

APPENDIX V--Objectives Roundtable Meetings 59

Abbreviations

AICPA	American Institute of Certified Public Accountants
CBO	Congressional Budget Office
CFO	Chief Financial Officer
FASAB	Federal Accounting Standards Advisory Board
FASB	Financial Accounting Standards Board
FFMIA	Federal Financial Management Improvement Act of 1996
GAAP	Generally Accepted Accounting Principles
GAGAS	Generally Accepted Government Auditing Standards
GAO	Government Accountability Office
GASB	Governmental Accounting Standards Board
GPRA	Government Performance and Results Act of 1993
IPSASB	International Public Sector Accounting Standards Board
MD&A	Management's Discussion and Analysis
NIPAs	National Income and Product Accounts
OCBOA	Other Comprehensive Basis of Accounting
OMB	Office of Management and Budget
PCIE	President's Council on Integrity and Efficiency
PMA	President's Management Agenda
SFFAC	Statement of Federal Financial Accounting Concepts
SFFAS	Statement of Federal Financial Accounting Standards
SOX	Sarbanes-Oxley Act of 2002

Executive Summary

During its initial years of operation, FASAB developed a core set of accounting standards and concepts statements. Now, after more than a dozen years of substantial progress, the Board believes that it is time to revisit the concepts given the changes in the federal financial reporting environment since the first concepts statement was issued. The objective of the Concepts Project is to ensure that federal financial accounting standards are based on a sound framework of objectives and concepts regarding the nature of accounting, financial statements, and other communications methods.

The Objectives phase of the overall Concepts Project related to the evaluation of the reporting objectives as presented in Statement of Federal Financial Accounting Concepts (SFFAC) 1, *Objectives of Federal Financial Reporting.* Evaluation of the reporting objectives focused on (1) clarifying the broad federal financial reporting objectives by determining if they are still valid and appropriate and whether additional objectives are necessary and (2) defining FASAB's strategic directions by clarifying its near-term role in achieving those broad objectives as the nature of the Board's involvement may vary for each objective. This document in essence serves as an update to cover developments in federal financial reporting since the issuance of SFFAC 1 and to define FASAB's strategic directions by clarifying the Board's near-term role relative to each reporting objective.

The Board believed that it would be beneficial to get feedback from the community on the reporting objectives given the changes in the environment over the past 10 years. During 2005, FASAB staff conducted separate roundtable discussions on each of the four reporting objectives. The participants agreed that the financial reporting objectives were very broad and related to a government-wide reform effort intended to improve the effectiveness and accountability of government. This reform effort engaged financial managers, budgeters, planners, evaluators, economists, systems experts, and auditors. Therefore, participants did not expect FASAB or financial statement reporting to cover or meet all the objectives alone. The Board agreed to maintain the current broad objectives of federal financial reporting in SFFAC 1.

Given the retention of the broad objectives of federal financial reporting, the Board determined it should articulate FASAB's strategic directions by clarifying the Board's near-term[1] role in relation to the broad objectives. The Board considered the following factors in defining the FASAB's strategic directions:

- Mission of FASAB;
- Current Language in Concepts Statements;

---

[1] Near-term is defined as approximately five years for the purposes of this document. In conjunction with strategic planning, FASAB may re-evaluate this assessment periodically.

- Comparative Advantages as a Generally Accepted Accounting Principles (GAAP) Standard-Setter;
- Evolution of Federal Financial Management and New Laws and Administrative Directives;
- Results from the Roundtable Meetings on each Objective; and,
- Other Factors such as Other Reports Fulfilling the Objectives and the Contribution of Current Standards.

Evaluating the objectives against the factors identified above **was an assessment to assist in determining FASAB's strategic directions in the near-term by defining FASAB's role in meeting each objective, <u>not</u> a ranking of the broad objectives.** Accordingly, FASAB assessed which objectives would provide more opportunity to play a direct role in achieving through accounting standards developed in the near-term. FASAB's assessment of the objectives is that there are two types of focus for FASAB in the near-term as follows:

Primary Near-Term Focus Objectives—Primary Near-Term Focus Objectives are those objectives where there is the greatest opportunity for FASAB to play a direct role by developing standards to achieve the stated objectives. Therefore, projects that support achieving Primary Near-Term Focus Objectives would be considered higher priorities in the near-term.

Secondary Near-Term Focus Objectives—Secondary Near-Term Focus Objectives are those objectives where there is not the greatest opportunity for FASAB to play a direct role by developing standards to achieve the stated objectives. In contrast to Primary Near-Term Focus Objectives, FASAB believes that for the most part it will play a supporting role in meeting these objectives in the near-term.

Illustration 1, FASAB's Strategic Directions: *Clarifying FASAB's Near-Term Role in Achieving the Objectives of Federal Financial Reporting* on page 1 provides a high-level pictorial of FASAB's role in relation to the Primary Near-Term Focus Objectives and Secondary Near-Term Focus Objectives. Illustration 2, *Analysis of Factors Considered in Clarifying FASAB's Near-Term Role* on page 14 provides a summary of the assessment of FASAB's role in achieving each objective for each consideration or factor by reporting objective. A detailed narrative explaining this assessment is included by reporting objective on pages 16 through 36.

The Board believes that Secondary Near-Term Focus Objectives may be re-prioritized as fundamental issues are resolved in the long-term. In the near-term, the Board believes that: 1) many of its active projects will address multiple objectives so that designation of a "secondary near-term focus" or "supporting role" objective does not preclude progress on meeting those objectives; and 2) it is possible that resources may become available to contribute to meeting a Secondary Near-Term Focus Objective.

Also, to implement the overall guidance provided by the strategic directions, the Board will continue to consider the following criteria in evaluating specific projects for its technical agenda:

1. Significance of the issue relative to meeting reporting objectives;
2. Pervasiveness of the issue among federal entities; and,
3. Technical outlook and resource needs.

Appendix I, *Criteria for Ranking Projects*, was adopted by the Board in October 2004 and provides additional information on each of these factors.

ILLUSTRATION 1 -- FASAB'S STRATEGIC DIRECTIONS:
Clarifying FASAB's Near-Term Role in Achieving the Objectives of Federal Financial Reporting

Budgetary Integrity

Federal financial reporting should assist in fulfilling the government's duty to be publicly accountable for monies raised through taxes and other means and for their expenditure in accordance with the appropriations laws that establish the government's budget for a particular fiscal year and related laws and regulations.

Operating Performance

Federal financial reporting should assist report users in evaluating the service efforts, costs, and accomplishments of the reporting entity; the manner in which these efforts and accomplishments have been financed; and the management of the entity's assets and liabilities.

Stewardship

Federal financial reporting should assist report users in assessing the impact on the country of the government's operations and investments for the period and how, as a result, the government's and the nation's financial condition has changed and may change in the future.

Systems and Control

Federal financial reporting should assist report users in understanding whether financial management systems and internal accounting and administrative controls are adequate...

Supporting Role

Direct Role

Direct Role

Supporting Role

Secondary Near-Term Focus

Board's Authority does not extend to Budgetary Measurement and Recognition

Other Reports Fulfilling Objective

Contr bution of Current Standards

Primary Near-Term Focus

Mission

Comparative Advantage/ GAAP Standards Setter

Language from Concepts 1

Secondary Near-Term Focus

Evolving Laws & Administrative Directives

Other Reports Fulfilling Objective

Contribution of Current Standards

FASAB'S ROLE

Introduction and Scope

During its initial years of operation, FASAB developed a core set of accounting standards and concepts statements. Now, after more than a dozen years of substantial progress, the Board believes that it is time to revisit the concepts given the changes in the federal financial reporting environment since the first concepts statement was issued. The objective of the Concepts Project is to ensure that federal financial accounting standards are based on a sound framework of objectives and concepts regarding the nature of accounting, financial statements, and other communications methods. The framework should:

- provide structure by describing the nature and limits of federal financial reporting;
- identify objectives that give direction to standard setters;
- define the elements critical to meeting financial reporting objectives and describe the statements used to present elements;
- identify means of communicating information necessary to meet objectives and describe when a particular means should be used; and,
- enable those affected by or interested in standards to better understand the purposes, content, and characteristics of information provided in federal financial reports.

The conceptual framework will refine and build on the current concepts promulgated by FASAB.

Objectives Phase of the Concepts Project - Evaluate Objectives

The Objectives phase of the overall Concepts Project related to the evaluation of the reporting objectives as presented in Statement of Federal Financial Accounting Concepts (SFFAC) 1, *Objectives of Federal Financial Reporting.* Evaluation of the reporting objectives focused on (1) clarifying the broad federal financial reporting objectives by determining if they are still valid and appropriate and whether additional objectives are necessary and (2) defining FASAB's strategic directions by clarifying its near-term role in achieving those broad objectives as the nature of the Board's involvement may vary for each objective.

The objective phase supported the Board's efforts to improve the conceptual framework and has been accomplished through the development of this document on objectives, drawing from the existing SFFAC 1 and other literature as needed. Developing this document assisted the Board in its efforts to (1) determine whether to amend or augment concepts statements regarding objectives of federal financial reporting and (2) define strategic directions. This document in essence serves as an update to cover developments in federal financial reporting since the issuance of SFFAC 1 and to define FASAB's strategic directions by clarifying the Board's near-term role relative to each reporting objective.

As the Board continues to take into account certain criteria when evaluating individual topics for its technical agenda,[2] the clarification of the objectives and defining the Board's near-term role relative to those objectives should (1) enhance the Board's selection of standards projects by making explicit the objectives most readily attainable through GAAP financial reports and (2) communicate to users FASAB's strategic directions.

SFFAC 1 Status

The Board relies on SFFAC 1 to support its deliberations on financial reporting issues. Briefly, SFFAC 1 discusses:

- Background information on federal financial reporting, its environment, and the role of the Board;
- User needs;
- Objectives;
- Cost and benefit considerations;
- Qualitative characteristics of information in financial reports; and,
- Relationships between accounting and financial reporting including operating performance.

SFFAC 1 acknowledges that many information sources other than financial statements help to attain the stated objectives. Further, SFFAC 1 does not assert that the Board will attempt to meet all the stated objectives. It simply states "FASAB will consider where new accounting standards could make a useful and cost-effective contribution to improving the extent to which these objectives are attained."

As noted above, the Board evaluated the objectives presented in chapter 4 of SFFAC 1 as part of the Objectives Phase of the Concepts Project. The objectives as stated in SFFAC 1 are as follows:

---

[2] See Appendix I, *Criteria for Ranking Projects*, for a discussion of the factors used in evaluating proposed projects for the technical agenda.

Objective 1--Budgetary Integrity

Federal financial reporting should assist in fulfilling the government's duty to be publicly accountable for monies raised through taxes and other means and for their expenditure in accordance with the appropriations laws that establish the government's budget for a particular fiscal year and related laws and regulations. *Federal financial reporting should provide information that helps the reader to determine:*

1A. How budgetary resources have been obtained and used and whether their acquisition and use were in accordance with the legal authorization.
1B. The status of budgetary resources.
1C. How information on the use of budgetary resources relates to information on the costs of program operations and whether information on the status of budgetary resources is consistent with other accounting information on assets and liabilities.

Objective 2--Operating Performance

Federal financial reporting should assist report users in evaluating the service efforts, costs, and accomplishments of the reporting entity; the manner in which these efforts and accomplishments have been financed; and the management of the entity's assets and liabilities. *Federal financial reporting should provide information that helps the reader to determine:*

2A. The costs of providing specific programs and activities and the composition of, and changes in, these costs.
2B. The efforts and accomplishments associated with federal programs and the changes over time and in relation to costs.
2C. The efficiency and effectiveness of the government's management of its assets and liabilities.

Objective 3--Stewardship

Federal financial reporting should assist report users in assessing the impact on the country of the government's operations and investments for the period and how, as a result, the government's and the nation's financial condition has changed and may change in the future. *Federal financial reporting should provide information that helps the reader to determine:*

3A. Whether the government's financial position improved or deteriorated over the period.
3B. Whether future budgetary resources will likely be sufficient to sustain public services and to meet obligations as they come due.
3C. Whether government operations have contributed to the nation's current and future well-being.

Objective 4--Systems and Control

Federal financial reporting should assist report users in understanding whether financial management systems and internal accounting and administrative controls are adequate to ensure that:

4A. Transactions are executed in accordance with budgetary and financial laws and other requirements, consistent with the purposes authorized, and are recorded in accordance with federal accounting standards;
4B. Assets are properly safeguarded to deter fraud, waste, and abuse; and
4C. Performance measurement information is adequately supported.

Defining FASAB's Strategic Directions by Clarifying the Board's Near-Term Role in Achieving the Broad Objectives of Financial Reporting

The Board considered the following factors in defining FASAB's strategic directions by clarifying the Board's near-tem role in achieving the broad objectives of financial reporting:

- Mission of FASAB;
- Current Language in Concepts Statements;
- Comparative Advantages as a GAAP Standard-Setter;
- Evolution of Federal Financial Management and New Laws and Administrative Directives;
- Results from the Roundtable Meetings on each Objective; and,
- Other Factors such as Other Reports Fulfilling the Objectives and the Contribution of Current Standards.

A high-level discussion of each factor is presented below. Illustration 1, FASAB's Strategic Directions: *Clarifying FASAB's Near-Term Role in Achieving the Objectives of Federal Financial Reporting* on page 1 provides a high-level pictorial of FASAB's role in relation to the Primary Near-Term Focus Objectives and Secondary Near-Term Focus Objectives. Illustration 2, *Analysis of Factors Considered in Clarifying FASAB's Near-Term Role* on page 14 provides a summary of the assessment for each consideration or factor by reporting objective. A detailed narrative explaining the assessment is included by reporting objective on pages 16 through 36.

Consideration of the Mission of FASAB

When defining FASAB's strategic directions and clarifying the Board's near-term role in relation to the broad objectives of federal financial reporting, FASAB's mission should be considered. FASAB's mission is referenced in SFFAC 1. However, a more detailed discussion regarding FASAB's mission can be found in the FASAB Facts (updated in 2006 and published on the web at http://www.fasab.gov/aboutfasab.html) as follows:

> The mission of the FASAB is to develop accounting standards [for the federal government] after considering the financial and budgetary information needs of congressional oversight groups, executive agencies, and the needs of other users of federal financial information.
>
> Accounting and financial reporting standards are essential for public accountability and for an efficient and effective functioning of our democratic system of government. Thus Federal accounting standards and financial reporting play a major role in fulfilling the government's duty to be publicly accountable and can be used to (1) assess the government's accountability and its efficiency and effectiveness, and (2) contribute to the understanding of the economic, political, and social consequences of the allocation and various uses of federal resources.

Accounting standards should:

- Result in the Federal Government and its agencies providing users of financial reports with understandable, relevant, and reliable information about the financial position, activities, and results of operations of the United States Government and its component units; and

- Foster the improvement of accounting systems and effective internal controls that will help provide reasonable assurance that governmental activities can be conducted economically, efficiently, and effectively, and in compliance with applicable laws and regulations.

Consideration of the Current Language in Concepts Statements

Definition of Financial Reporting

Additionally, the definition of 'financial reporting' should be considered in establishing FASAB's near-term role in relation to the broad objectives of financial reporting. SFFAC 1 recognizes "different people are likely to talk about very different things when asked to describe federal financial reporting or federal accounting."[3] SFFAC 1 par. 21-22 describes financial reporting as follows:

21. Financial reporting by the federal government provides information for formulating policy, planning actions, evaluating performance, and other purposes. In addition, the processes of preparing and auditing financial reports can enhance the government's overall accountability structure by providing greater assurance that transactions are recorded and reported accurately, that consistent definitions are used to describe the transactions, etc. Thus, federal financial reporting helps to fulfill the government's duty to manage programs economically, efficiently, and effectively and to be publicly accountable.

22. Financial reporting is supported and made possible by accounting and accounting systems. "Financial reporting" may be defined as the process of recording, reporting, and interpreting, in terms of money, an entity's financial transactions and events with economic consequences for the entity. Reporting in the federal government also deals with nonfinancial information about service efforts and accomplishments of the government, i.e., the inputs of resources used by the government, the outputs of goods and services provided by the government, the outcomes and impacts of governmental programs, and the relationships among these elements.

Limitations of Financial Reporting

SFFAC 1, par. 106 also recognizes that financial reporting is not the only source of information by stating: "Financial reporting is not the only source of information to

---

[3] SFFAC 1, par. 38

support decision-making and accountability. Neither can financial reporting, by itself, ensure that the government operates as it should. Financial reporting can, however, make a useful contribution toward those objectives."

SFFAC 1 also describes the reporting methods and the need for general purpose financial reports, special reports and other reports in meeting the objectives and needs of users. It also addresses FASAB's ability to consider the issues involved in the reports. SFFAC par. 31 – 34 state:

31. While certain information is provided by general purpose financial reports, other information is better provided by, or can be provided only by, financial reporting outside such reports. Still other information is provided by nonfinancial reports or by financial reports about segments of the national society other than the federal government and its component entities (e.g., economic reporting).

32. Often, to satisfy the information needs of various individuals, it is necessary to combine and report financial and nonfinancial information. Often, combining information about the government with information about aspects of the national society is necessary to assess past or planned governmental actions. For example, information about the number of people gainfully employed after participating in a vocational education program would be important both in assessing past governmental expenditures for training and in evaluating plans for similar new expenditures.

33. Some questions arise with special force regarding the nature of general purpose reports because, by definition, no user or potential user is able unilaterally to define the requirements for these reports. The FASAB is, by design, well constituted to consider the issues involved with such reports.

34. Federal accounting also must support special purpose reporting to the Congress, executives, and others that the FASAB represents. Indeed, most federal financial reporting is special purpose reporting. Also, the Board notes that traditional "general purpose" financial reports may serve a larger and more useful purpose for a variety of audiences if traditional designs for such reports are expanded to include a variety of reports addressing budgetary integrity, operating performance, stewardship, and control of federal activities.

SFFAC 1 describes the objectives as a broad statement of federal financial reporting objectives and not limited to objectives to be met by the development of accounting standards. Specifically FASAB recognized its own limitations, and that other sources of information are important to achieving the objectives in SFFAC 1 par. 35-37 as follows:

35. The FASAB recognizes that developing and implementing standards that will contribute to achieving certain objectives may take considerable time. Time will be needed to establish information-gathering systems and to gain experience by experimenting with alternative approaches.

36. The FASAB expects that some of these objectives may best be accomplished through means of reporting outside general purpose financial reports. Indeed the

FASAB recognizes that information sources other than financial reporting, sources over which the FASAB may have little or no influence, also are important to achieving the goals implied by these objectives.

37. In developing specific standards, the FASAB will consider the needs of financial information users, the usefulness of the information in relation to the cost of developing and providing it, and the ability of accounting standards to address those needs compared with other information sources.

SFFAC 1 and SFFAC 2, *Entity and Display*, do not envision a narrowly defined "general purpose financial report." References to combining financial and non-financial information are common. For example, SFFAC 2 recognizes the need for a statement of program performance and refers to such a statement as "not only an appropriate financial statement, but likely to be the most important financial statement for those persons interested in how a federal entity is using its resources."[4] Additionally, the detailed assessment of FASAB's near-term role in achieving each objective contains references to additional language within the Concepts Statements.

Consideration of the Comparative Advantages as a GAAP Standard-Setter

FASAB has evolved since it was created in 1990. Most notably, in October 1999, the American Institute of Certified Public Accountants' (AICPA) Council designated the FASAB as the accounting standards-setting body for federal government entities under Rule 203 of the AICPA's Code of Professional Conduct. Rule 203 provides, in part, that an AICPA member shall not (1) express an opinion or state affirmatively that the financial statements or other financial data of any entity are presented in conformity with GAAP or (2) state that he or she is not aware of any material modifications that should be made to such statements or data in order for them to be in conformity with GAAP, if such statements or data contain any departure from an accounting principle promulgated by bodies designated by Council to establish such principles, that has a material effect on the statements or data taken as a whole. (See Appendix II, *Evolution in FASAB*, for a complete description of the evolution in FASAB and other changes.)

FASAB's designation as a GAAP standards-setter does offer a comparative advantage that is unique in federal financial reporting. With this designation, federal reporting entities obtain audit opinions that indicate that the financial statements are fairly presented in conformity with GAAP. The GAAP designation enhances federal financial reporting in these respects:

- *Credibility*--GAAP recognition, with continued monitoring by the accounting profession, indicates that the Board meets the minimum requirements for a financial reporting standards-setting body. These are Independence, Due

---

[4] SFFAC 2, par. 66

Process and Standards, Domain and Authority, Human and Financial Resources, and Comprehensiveness and Consistency.

■ *Ability to set a common framework for debate and offer a forum for consideration of financial reporting issues*--While it does not limit the Board's role, GAAP status demands comprehensiveness and consistency. Thus, GAAP standards-setters endeavor to establish a sound conceptual framework, address critical issues in a timely manner, and introduce discipline to financial measures. Through development of, continual improvement in, and application of financial accounting concepts and standards, GAAP governs the terms used in financial discussions and the financial representation given to transactions and events.

The Board follows due process under Rule 203. Thus, the Board must continue to conduct outreach and consider the views of those interested in federal financial reporting. This is both a responsibility and an opportunity. Also, as part of its outreach efforts, the Board monitors the activities of other standards-setting authorities, such as the International Public Sector Accounting Standards Board (IPSASB), and seeks their views on proposed concepts and standards. Because of due process, the Board is challenged to produce concepts and standards that are defensible and understandable. Further, the Board may use due process as a means to engage users of reports and members of the various professions having an interest in federal finances. Through the Board's efforts, public policy and budget experts may engage in financial accounting/reporting deliberations. This creates the opportunity to produce more useful and understandable concepts and standards for financial reporting.

■ *Impact on external decision makers through ability to require unbiased information (to send "bad news") due to independence*--Independence has been identified as the most significant criterion for a GAAP standards-setter. With an independent standard-setter it is more likely that government organizations will be required to provide a complete financial report including "bad news."

FASAB's influence on federal financial reporting is unique. The Board determines financial reporting concepts and standards through an extensive and widely participative due process that emphasizes user needs as embodied in the reporting objectives. Federal entities follow these standards in preparing financial statements subject to independent audit. Independent auditors determine whether the financial statements are presented fairly in accordance with GAAP, which encompasses those concepts, standards, and practices required to define accepted accounting principles at a particular time.

Audited financial statements based on GAAP have an advantage in meeting users' needs in several ways. For example, the discipline introduced through audited financial statement preparation and through established definition, recognition, and measurement guidance can lead to enhanced systems and processes, and ultimately more reliable information. Also, internal reporting and analyses are enhanced along with focusing attention on areas of concern. Consequently, users can gain a level of assurance that the information they utilize is accurate.

In addition, the information provided in financial statements meets users' needs because it demonstrates accountability and may be useful for decision-making. For example, knowledge that certain information will be made publicly available can have behavioral consequences, such as deterring fraud, waste, and abuse. It also may lead reporters, analysts, and others to expect certain information (outside of the Budget) on a routine schedule. Also, managers may desire to inform Congress of information that is not included in the Budget. Consequently, information can be made available to demonstrate accountability and that can be useful for decision-making.

In addition, GAAP reports provide an advantage because the information in such reports must possess certain characteristics that help to effectively communicate information to users. SFFAC 1 describes six characteristics that the information must possess-- Understandability, Reliability, Relevance, Timeliness, Consistency, and Comparability.[5]

All of the foregoing adds a degree of credibility and acceptability to FASAB's standards that may not exist elsewhere in the federal jurisdiction. Although there may be other reporting requirements (other than financial statements) that are contributing to achieving certain objectives, information required by a FASAB standard brings a level of assurance about the reliability of the information because it is subject to due process and audit. See Appendix III, *GAAP and Non-GAAP Reporting*.

Consideration of the Evolution of Federal Financial Management and New Laws and Administrative Directives

The Chief Financial Officers (CFO) Act could be considered the first of a series of major legislation passed beginning in 1990 to improve federal accountability through financial management reform. Briefly, the purposes of the CFO Act were to (1) bring more effective financial management practices to the federal government, (2) provide for the production of complete, reliable, and consistent financial information for use in management and evaluation of federal programs, and (3) improve agency systems of accounting, financial management, and internal controls.

Since then, and following in the steps of the CFO Act, Congress has enacted a series of laws to reform and improve financial management in the federal government. Along the lines of the three purposes of the CFO Act described in the previous paragraph, the legislation enacted and related administrative directives issued since 1993 broadly fall into three areas:

---

[5] See SFFAC 1 par. 156-164 for discussion of the Qualitative Characteristics of Information in Financial Reports.

- **Effective Financial Management Practices**--Legislation and administrative directives to bring more effective financial management practices to the federal government;
- **Performance Measurement**--Legislation and administrative directives to provide for the production of complete, reliable, and consistent financial information for use in management and evaluation of federal programs; and
- **Internal Controls**--Legislation and administrative directives to improve agency systems of accounting, financial management, and internal controls.

Accordingly, it would be appropriate to consider these and the related changes in the federal financial reporting environment since SFFAC 1 was issued in 1993.

The recent legislation and administrative directives related to *Effective Financial Management Practices* include: Government Management Reform Act of 1994, Reports Consolidation Act of 2000, Accountability of Tax Dollars Act of 2002, Improper Payments Information Act of 2002, and the President's Management Agenda *Improved Financial Performance Initiative*. Some legislation and administrative directives in this area focused on extending requirements of the CFO Act for audited financial statements from the original CFO agencies to other agencies as well as the consolidated government-wide financial statements. Legislation and administrative directives also focused on streamlining reporting requirements by allowing agencies to produce a Performance and Accountability Report. Additionally, agencies are issuing more timely financial reports due to the accelerated due dates. Agency efforts to comply with the legislation and administrative directives in this area have brought about more effective financial management practices, but do not appear to significantly contribute to meeting any one objective that would impact the assessment of FASAB's focus.

The recent legislation and administrative directives related to *Performance Measurement* include: Government Performance and Results Act of 1993, President's Management Agenda *Budget and Performance Integration Initiative*, and OMB's Program Assessment Rating Tool Analysis. The legislation and administrative directives noted in this area focused on the production of complete and reliable performance information for use in management and evaluation of federal programs. It appears that most of the legislation and administrative directives in this area have a direct relationship with the Operating Performance Objective. In particular, they relate to this sub-objective: 'The efforts and accomplishments associated with federal programs and the changes over time and in relation to costs.' Agency efforts to comply with the legislation and administrative directives in this area (and the resulting oversight by OMB) seem to significantly contribute to meeting this sub-objective related to performance measurement. The extent to which this sub-objective is addressed through other means impacts the assessment of FASAB's focus on this particular sub-objective.

The recent legislation and administrative directives related to *Internal Controls* include: Federal Managers' Financial Integrity Act of 1982[6], Federal Financial Management Improvement Act of 1996 (FFMIA), Sarbanes-Oxley Act of 2002 (SOX), OMB Circular A-123 (REVISED December 2004) *Management's Responsibility for Internal Control*, Department of Homeland Security Financial Accountability Act, and the President's Management Agenda *Improved Financial Performance Initiative*. The legislation and administrative directives noted in this area focused on the improvement of agency systems of accounting, financial management, and internal controls. It appears that most of the legislation and administrative directives in this area have a direct relationship with the Systems and Control Objective. Agency efforts to comply with the legislation and administrative directives in this area (and the resulting oversight by OMB) seem to significantly contribute to meeting certain aspects of the Systems and Control Objective. The extent to which this objective is addressed through other means impacts the assessment of FASAB's focus on this particular objective. Accordingly, GAAP standards promulgated by FASAB to meet the Systems and Control Objective do not appear to be a high priority at this time.

A detailed summary and analysis of the impact of each pertinent law and administrative directive is presented in Appendix IV, *Evolutions in Federal Financial Management and Reporting Laws and Administrative Directives since the CFO Act of 1990*.

Consideration of the Results from Roundtable Meetings on each Objective

The Board believed that it would be beneficial to get feedback from the community on the reporting objectives given the changes in the environment over the past 10 years. During 2005, FASAB staff conducted separate roundtable discussions on each of the four reporting objectives. The primary purpose of the discussions was to determine how each objective might be improved to facilitate its use as a means for guiding the board in developing standards of financial accounting and reporting and in developing solutions to financial accounting and reporting issues.

From the Roundtable meetings, the Board learned that participants at all roundtables believe that the financial reporting objectives, although broad, are still valid today. Overall, the participants agreed that the financial reporting objectives were very broad, but they did not expect FASAB or financial statement reporting to cover or meet all the objectives alone. This was consistent with the Board's view that information sources other than financial statements help to attain the objectives. The participants viewed the SFFAC 1 objectives as a broad statement of federal financial reporting objectives and not limited to objectives to be met by the development of accounting standards. Although the participants did offer areas for improvement, there was no indication that any objective should be removed or revised. The participants believed that the federal financial reporting objectives should remain broad and that if FASAB wishes to

---

[6] Although FMFIA came before the CFO Act of 1990, it is included as it is relevant for understanding how other requirements achieve the Systems and Control objective.

document its focus, it should be done in a manner that would not limit the Board or eliminate any objective in SFFAC 1.

A brief summary of each of the roundtable meetings is provided in Appendix V, *Objectives Roundtable Meetings*.

Staff presented the results of the Roundtable meetings to the Board at the March 2006 Board meeting. The Board members discussed whether the federal financial reporting objectives should remain broad and the Board noted that FASAB does appear to have a comparative advantage in stating the objectives of federal financial reporting. The Board agreed to maintain the current broad objectives of federal financial reporting and that FASAB should not eliminate objectives in SFFAC 1.

Consideration of Other Factors such as Other Reports Fulfilling the Objectives and the Contribution of Current Standards

It would be appropriate to consider that there are other current reports and reporting requirements that provide information that assist in achieving the objectives.[7] For example, the *Budget of the United States Government* is considered the government's principal financial report and provides much of the information necessary to meet the Budgetary Integrity objective. In addition, existing FASAB standards contribute to achieving certain aspects of the objectives. While FASAB acknowledges the broad, non-traditional vision embodied in SFFACs 1 and 2, the Board considered the following other factors in defining its near-term role in relation to the broad objectives:

- the ability of accounting standards to address information needs compared with other information sources;
- the interrelated nature of the reporting objectives and whether there are foundational issues that, when resolved, facilitate meeting other objectives; and,
- the contribution of current standards to meeting reporting objectives.

---

[7] However, reporting information in non-GAAP statements is not an acceptable substitute for information required for fair presentation in GAAP financial statements. See Appendix III for a discussion of GAAP and Non-GAAP reporting.

ILLUSTRATION 2 -- Analysis of Factors Considered in Clarifying FASAB's Near-Term Role

Considerations/ Factors	Budgetary Integrity Objective	Operating Performance Objective	Stewardship Objective	Systems and Control Objective
FASAB's Mission/ MOU	Supporting Role	Direct Role	Direct Role	Supporting Role
Language from SFFAC 1	Supporting Role	Direct Role	Direct Role	Supporting Role
Comparative Advantage/ GAAP	Supporting Role	Direct Role	Direct Role	Supporting Role
New Laws & Admin. Directives	No Effect	Supporting Role	No Effect	Supporting Role
Roundtable Meetings	Supporting Role	Direct Role	Supporting Role	Supporting Role
Other Reports Fulfilling Objective	Supporting Role	Direct Role	Supporting Role	Supporting Role
Contribution of Current Standards	Supporting Role	Direct Role	Direct Role	Supporting Role

Legend:

Direct Role	**Direct Role** - After consideration of the factor, FASAB would have the greatest opportunity to play a direct role by developing standards to achieve the stated objective in the near-term.
Supporting Role	**Supporting Role** - After consideration of the factor, FASAB would NOT have the greatest opportunity to play a direct role by developing standards to achieve the stated objective in the near-term. In contrast, FASAB believes it will play a supporting or secondary role in the near-term in meeting these objectives.
No Effect	**No Effect** - After consideration of the factor, there is no impact on the assessment of FASAB's role in achieving the objective.

Assessment of FASAB's Near-Term Role in Achieving Each Objective

In assessing the objectives, the Board considered language from SFFAC 1, discussions at roundtables held during 2005, and current reporting – including current GAAP reports and other reports - that contribute to meeting the objective. One of the main purposes of this project was to define FASAB's strategic directions by clarifying the Board's near-term role in achieving the broad objectives, as the nature of the Board's involvement may vary for each objective.

Defining FASAB's role in meeting each objective was an assessment to assist in determining FASAB's strategic directions in the near-term, not a ranking of the broad objectives. Accordingly, FASAB assessed which objectives would provide more opportunity to play a direct role in achieving through accounting standards developed in the near-term. Illustration 2, *Analysis of Factors Considered in Clarifying FASAB's Near-Term Role* on page 14 provides a summary of this assessment for each consideration or factor by reporting objective. A detailed narrative explaining this assessment is included by reporting objective on pages 16 through 36. FASAB's assessment of the objectives is that there are two types of focus for FASAB in the near-term[8] as follows:

Primary Near-Term Focus Objectives—Primary Near-Term Focus Objectives are those objectives where there is the greatest opportunity for FASAB to play a direct role by developing standards to achieve the stated objectives. Therefore, projects that support achieving Primary Near-Term Focus Objectives would be considered higher priorities in the near-term.

Secondary Near-Term Focus Objectives—Secondary Near-Term Focus Objectives are those objectives where there is not the greatest opportunity for FASAB to play a direct role by developing standards to achieve the stated objectives. In contrast to Primary Near-Term Focus Objectives, FASAB believes that for the most part it will play a supporting role in meeting these objectives in the near-term.

However, the Board believes that Secondary Near-Term Focus Objectives may be re-prioritized as fundamental issues are resolved in the long-term. In the near-term, the Board believes that many of its active projects will address multiple objectives so that designation of a "secondary near-term focus" or "supporting role" objective does not preclude progress on meeting those objectives. For example, a project focused on the Operating Performance Objective may indirectly contribute to meeting the Systems and Control Objective. Further, it is possible that resources may become available to contribute to meeting a Secondary Near-Term Focus Objective. A detailed explanation of the factors considered in determining the focus for each objective follows.

---

[8] Near-term is defined as approximately five years for the purposes of this document. In conjunction with strategic planning, FASAB may re-evaluate this assessment periodically.

FASAB's Primary Near-Term Focus Objectives

Based on the assessment and consideration of the factors noted above, FASAB determined its Primary Near-Term Focus Objectives are the Operating Performance Objective and the Stewardship Objective. Among the two Primary Near-Term Focus Objectives, the Board believes the Operating Performance Objective to be its top priority. FASAB believes that making it the top priority allows for progress on all of the objectives because of the interrelated nature of the reporting objectives. A summary of the factors supporting placing these two objectives as Primary Near-Term Focus Objectives is below.

Operating Performance

The Operating Performance Objective is FASAB's top priority at the present time and the one where there is greatest opportunity to play a direct role in developing standards that would achieve the objective. Most would agree that the Operating Performance Objective relates to integrating cost information derived from accrual accounting with performance reporting. In addition, it addresses the financing of efforts, creating a link to budgetary resources, changes in assets and liabilities over time, and financial sustainability reporting. Information about the assets and liabilities of the government also provides a foundation for meeting the Stewardship Objective which calls first for information about the financial position of the government. Placing the Operating Performance Objective as a top priority allows for progress on all of the objectives because of the interrelated nature of the reporting objectives.

With respect to the Stewardship Objective, SFFAC 1, par. 137 states that "analysis of *why* financial position improved or deteriorated helps explain whether financial burdens were passed on by current-year taxpayers to future-year taxpayers without related benefits." In addition, while Stewardship sub-objective 3B (..whether future budgetary resources will likely be sufficient to sustain public services and to meet obligations as they come due) appears to call for projections, the narrative related to the sub-objective explains that "information about the results of past government operations is useful in assessing the stewardship exercised by the government." Examples of information relevant to the sub-objective are (1) financial risks from government-sponsored enterprises, deposit insurance, and disaster relief programs, (2) the long-term financial implications of the budgetary process, (3) the status of trust funds, and (4) backlogs of deferred maintenance. Many – if not all - of the above examples relate to reporting on financial position. Thus, a thorough assessment of financial position is essential to meeting (but not sufficient to meet) Operating Performance and Stewardship Objectives.

Developing standards for achieving the Operating Performance Objective should be considered a top priority based on the factors discussed below--language found in SFFAC 1, FASAB's comparative advantage in this area, and results from the Roundtable meetings. In addition, considering that the Operating Performance Objective addresses several sub-objectives that are related, but suggest different reporting outcomes, one could rank the sub-objectives. In particular, the impact of new laws and administrative directives on FASAB's focus on the sub-objectives is discussed below.

FASAB's Mission

When evaluating FASAB's mission, one could point out that the mission does in essence provide some narrowing by identifying FASAB's role in relation to 'accounting standards.' SFFAC 1 further states in par. 26 that: "The FASAB was created to advise OMB and Treasury (agents of the President) and the GAO (an agent of the Congress) on accounting standards for federal agencies and programs in order to improve financial reporting practices."

Further support of FASAB's focus on accounting is explained in SFFAC 1, Chapter 7 *How Accounting Supports Federal Financial Reporting*. Par. 165 states "This chapter explains the focus of the FASAB's concern by showing how accounting supports financial reporting and thus how accounting standards recommended by the FASAB can influence federal financial reporting. This chapter shows how the FASAB's recommendations can influence a wide variety of financial reports...."

Language from SFFAC 1

SFFAC 1 describes that most accountants, auditors and accounting students typically think about proprietary accounts and reports prepared from them when considering financial reporting. SFFAC 1 describes that FASAB is most directly concerned with these accounts in par. 47, which states "These accounts are used to record assets and liabilities that are not accounted for in the budgetary accounts. These reports are said to present "financial position" and "results of operations" in accordance with some set of accounting standards. The FASAB is most directly concerned with these accounts and with the reports that are prepared, in large part, with information from them."

In addition, par. 191 describes the Board's focus as: "The Board's own focus is on developing generally accepted accounting standards for reporting on the financial operations, financial position, and financial condition of the federal government and its component entities and other useful financial information..." As such, most would also see this as meaning that perhaps FASAB is most directly concerned with the Operating Performance objective because it relates most closely with these types of items— assets, liabilities, and results.

SFFAC 2, *Entity and Display*, recognized that each reporting objective could be achieved through different reporting. Par. 56 of SFFAC 2 states "The objective of operating performance can be best met with financial statements from organizations / sub-organizations and programs..." The Statement of Net Cost was designed with that in mind and calls for presentation of net cost by responsibility segment and program. SFFAC 2, par. 66, further suggests that a statement of program performance is "an appropriate financial statement." On balance, SFFAC 1 envisions a financial report that includes non-financial performance information. SFFAC 1 and 2 seem to suggest a role for FASAB in ensuring that financial information about costs, assets and liabilities is integrated with performance information. With respect to non-financial information, FASAB has provided for summary performance information in the MD&A but has not addressed a statement of program performance.

FASAB's Comparative Advantage

During its deliberations, the Board has acknowledged the comparative advantages of federal accounting in general and of GAAP reporting in particular. One advantage in particular is that users can gain a level of assurance that the information they utilize is consistent and comprehensive. Also, the discipline of preparing financial statements for audit can lead to improved government systems and processes. The section "Consideration of the Comparative Advantages as a GAAP Standards Setter" (see page 8) discusses FASAB's comparative advantage in more detail.

In addition, the Board has noted that financial statements are the principal means of communicating accounting information about an entity's resources, obligations, revenues, and costs to those outside the entity. Considering that a primary objective of the federal government is to provide services, a financial statement should communicate to citizens how much of the services were financed by taxpayers. A Statement of Net Cost communicates this information and supports achievement of the Operating Performance objective. Other financial statements, such as a Statement of Changes in Net Position help citizens understand the manner in which net costs were financed and the effect on the government entity's net position. Thus, the Statement of

Changes in Net Position also contributes to achieving the Operating Performance objective.[9]

Roundtable Meetings

The Operating Performance roundtable participants described this objective as very important and believed it is vital that agencies continue to make progress in all areas at achieving this objective. The participants noted that while there is a need to maintain high standards, agencies are still having difficulty meeting basic financial reporting requirements as well as this objective. Additionally, the participants noted that agencies continue to struggle with determining what information should be conveyed and that there is still a need for improvement in understanding how the information relates and utilizing it in decision-making. The participants also believed that integrating financial and performance systems and consequences for not controlling costs may help change behavior and begin to address some of the challenges. Further, the participants discussed that FASAB could have a role in education and providing non-authoritative guidance.

In addition, participants at the roundtable meetings for the other objectives, echoed concerns that there are still very basic accounting issues that need to be addressed by the Board and there is much progress to be made by agencies in basic accounting areas that could be viewed to relate to or be addressed in the Operating Performance Objective. Specifically, certain participants offered that FASAB, with its limited resources, should focus on addressing the direct technical accounting issues that remain.

Overall, the operating performance roundtable discussion suggests that FASAB may wish to offer leadership regarding the integration of financial and non-financial information while developing additional standards that support determination of full cost and financial position. A brief summary of each of the roundtable meetings is provided in Appendix V, Objectives Roundtable Meetings.

---

[9] SFFAC 2, paragraphs 59 and 60.

> **Changes in the Environment due to New Laws and Administrative Directives**

Considering that the Operating Performance Objective addresses several sub-objectives that are related[10] but suggest different reporting outcomes, one could rank the sub-objectives. This ranking[11] could potentially be in the following order:

1. The efficiency and effectiveness of the government's management of its assets and liabilities.
2. The costs of providing specific programs and activities and the composition of, and changes in, these costs.
3. The efforts and accomplishments associated with federal programs and the changes over time and in relation to costs.

This ranking of sub-objectives would be appropriate after consideration of the evolution of federal financial reporting laws and administrative directives and the changes in the environment resulting. As mentioned earlier in this document, since the CFO Act, Congress has enacted a series of laws to reform and improve financial management in the federal government. It was noted that there were several new laws that contributed to effective financial management practices, such as extending the requirements of the CFO Act, streamlining reporting requirements, and requiring timely reporting.

It was also noted that there were several new laws and administrative directives related to performance information (such as the Government Performance Results Act (GPRA), President's Management Agenda (PMA), and Program Assessment Rating Tool (PART)) that focused on the production of complete and reliable performance information for use in management and evaluation of federal programs. It appears that most of the new laws and administrative directives in this area have a direct relationship with the Operating Performance Sub-objective: 'The efforts and accomplishments associated with federal programs and the changes over time and in relation to costs.' Agency efforts to comply with laws and administrative directives (and the resulting oversight by OMB) may significantly contribute to meeting many aspects of the sub-objective. The extent to which this sub-objective is addressed through other means impacts the assessment of FASAB's focus on this particular sub-objective. Also, many of the new requirements, such as the PART, are very new and the ultimate benefit and effect on performance reporting is not known. Therefore, it would be appropriate that the focus of

---

[10] For example, costs cannot be determined absent recognition of assets and liabilities. In addition, efficiency of managing assets suggests an assessment of the cost associated with holding, using or preserving assets.

[11] Ranking of the sub-objectives for the Operating Performance Objective was to assist in defining FASAB's role in the near-term, not a ranking of the sub-objectives.

this particular sub-objective would be lower (when compared to the other Operating Performance sub-objectives) as this area continues to evolve.

A detailed summary and analysis of the impact of each pertinent law and administrative directive is presented in Appendix IV, *Evolutions in Federal Financial Management and Reporting Laws and Administrative Directives since the CFO Act of 1990*.

Stewardship

The Stewardship Objective is based on the government's responsibility for the general welfare of the nation. The Stewardship Objective is the broadest of all the objectives. Many aspects of this objective are important to citizens and FASAB does consider it a Primary Near-Term Focus Objective. However, it may not be considered FASAB's 'top priority' (when compared to the Operating Performance Objective) for the reasons discussed below—language from SFFAC 1, results from the roundtable meetings, other reports fulfilling this objective, and current FASAB standards and concepts statements.

Language from SFFAC 1

SFFAC 1 provides a brief discussion on economic financial reporting and notes that most reports of this type would address the national society as a whole and national income and product accounts (NIPAs). It further describes that NIPAs provide vital information to policymakers and are an essential part of economic reporting by national governments.

SFFAC 1 par. 42 clarifies FASAB's role and the objectives in relation to the economic reports as follows:

42.   This Statement does not deal directly with such accounts of the economic activity of the national society. The focus of this Statement is on accounting systems and financial reports that deal with the budgetary integrity, operating performance, and stewardship of the government as such; that is, of the government as a legal and organizational entity within the national society. However, to report on some aspects of the government's performance and stewardship, economic and other information about the national society is essential. Thus, the FASAB may consider whether such economic information should be included in certain financial reports, such as general purpose financial reports for the U.S. government as a whole.

Consequently, the "FASAB may consider whether such economic information should be included in certain financial reports, such as general purpose financial reports for the U.S. government as a whole," and "federal financial reporting cannot by itself accomplish the objectives of evaluating or assuring stewardship; it can only contribute to those goals."[12]

The Board recognized that the focus of the stewardship objective was broader than the other objectives as par. 135 of SFFAC 1 states: "This objective is based on the federal government's responsibility for the general welfare of the nation in perpetuity. It focuses not on the provision of specific services but on the requirement that the government report the broad outcomes of its actions..." In addition, the Basis for Conclusions provides additional reasoning for the broad focus and recognition of two levels of stewardship:

> 236. The Board notes that the federal government has two levels of stewardship. One is for its own assets and liabilities and its ongoing ability to operate. The other is its constitutional responsibility for the nation's wealth and well-being. It is unique in this respect. If the nation's wealth and well-being are deteriorating, the government's financial condition is, or soon will be, deteriorating also and vice versa. The financial condition of a sovereign national government and that of the nation itself are inextricably intertwined. Some information about the overall context must be provided, therefore, when reporting on the government as a whole, and perhaps when reporting on selected programs. As explained in chapter 1 the FASAB does not recommend standards for economic reporting, but it may consider whether such information should be included in certain financial reports.

Roundtable Meetings

Although most participants at the Stewardship Roundtable believed that FASAB has an advantage in developing a reporting framework that fairly presents the financial condition of the federal government, the participants noted that much of the information needed to fulfill the Stewardship Objective is developed outside of FASAB's domain. The participants discussed that FASAB could say that certain information is important and fits the framework that should be filled out, but the specifics of the information should be left up to others. For this and other objectives, the participants commented

---

[12] SFFAC 1, par. 235

that a combination of accounting and other data are essential for a full assessment of whether the objective is met.

The participants also discussed that the Stewardship Objective relates to the nation as a whole. The participants explained that when looking at the nation as a whole, wealth includes all sectors, and draws on the NIPAs, Flow of Funds Balance Sheets, and data on total investment in education and R&D. The participants discussed that the wealth of the nation is more than the federal government and the participants believed that developing standards for these measures is not the role of FASAB.

A participant stated, "I think some of this discussion is interesting, but I think for purposes of what is FASAB's mission and where its standard-setting resources should be targeted, it is kind of out in somebody else's domain." The participants noted that many of the issues relative to the Stewardship Objective are subject to political debate and that is where they should be debated. The participants noted that this is an important area, but may not be a role for an accounting standards board. However, the participants believed that FASAB could make a contribution by providing reporting concepts that fairly present financial condition and sustainability, accounting standards that have a complementary role in analyzing financial condition, and support for the transparency and validity of data.

Based on the discussions of the roundtable participants, it does not appear that the Stewardship Objective would be considered FASAB's top priority among its Primary Near-Term Focus Objectives. Nonetheless, as explained under the Operating Performance Objective, substantial progress can be made toward meeting the Stewardship Objective through enhanced information about financial position. In addition, resources would remain available to contribute to meeting this objective.

A brief summary of each of the roundtable meetings is provided in Appendix V, Objectives Roundtable Meetings.

Other Reports Fulfilling this Objective

There are several other current reports that provide information to fulfill the Stewardship Objective. SFFAC 1, Appendix C: Selected Federal Reports Prepared on a Recurring Basis, lists the *Budget of the U.S. Government* as one of several reports that contributes to meeting the financial reporting objectives. The *Analytical Perspectives* section of the *Budget of the U.S. Government* provides a chapter on Stewardship, which focuses on reviewing the condition of the federal government in relation to the national economy. This chapter is intended to meet the interests of economists and others in evaluating past and future trends. It notes that no single statistic encompasses all the factors that affect the financial condition of the federal government. Instead, the federal government's fiscal status should be evaluated using a broad range of data and complementary perspectives. The Stewardship chapter provides information on how the government affects national economic and social conditions, and it provides data to indicate the scope of the government's future responsibilities and the resources it will have available to discharge them under current law and policy. The chapter presents some economic and social indicators such as median income, civilian unemployment, poverty rate, air quality, violent crime rate, and life expectancy. Other reports that contribute to the objective include Congressional Budget Office's (CBO) Analysis of the President's Budget, which discusses the budgetary impact of the proposals in the President's budget and the Budget and Economic Outlook Report, which discusses the state of the budget and the economy.

FASAB's Current Standards and Other Concepts Statements

In addition to other reports, SFFAC 3, *Management's Discussion and Analysis*, and SFFAS 15, *Management's Discussion and Analysis*, require a Management's Discussion and Analysis that is forward-looking. The SFFAC 3 description of the information relevant to meeting the Stewardship Objective is shown below:

32. <u>Future Effects of Current Demands, Risks, Uncertainties, Events, Conditions and Trends</u>—The discussion of these current factors should go beyond a mere description of existing conditions, such as demographic characteristics, claims, deferred maintenance, commitments [13] undertaken, and major unfunded liabilities, to include a discussion of the possible future effect of those factors. (This discussion of possible future <u>effect</u> of existing, currently-known factors is required pursuant to the standards in *Standards for Management's Discussion and Analysis*.[SFFAS 15]) (footnote 13 - The term "commitments" is used here in the customary sense, not as it is used in budgetary accounting.)

33. <u>Future Effects of Anticipated Future Events, Conditions, and Trends</u>—To the extent feasible and appropriate, the discussion should also encompass the possible future effects of <u>anticipated future</u> events, conditions, and trends, although this additional information is not required by the standards for MD&A.[14] For example, MD&A might discuss the possible future effect of anticipated trends in the cost of inputs that may significantly affect future output costs. Other examples include the future effect of anticipated demographic trends, such as declining mortality rates, and the future effects of potential changes in behavior that may be caused by changes in Government programs. Such behavioral changes can greatly affect the future cost of some Governmental programs. For example, such effects can arise if subsidized insurance encourages the people or entities most at risk to participate in insurance programs ("adverse selection") or encourages risky behavior ("moral hazard").

[footnote 14 - Some projections that could involve consideration of anticipated factors would be presented as required supplementary stewardship information pursuant to the standards exposed for comment in FASAB's exposure draft Accounting for Social Insurance, February, 1998.]

34. An anticipated condition such as a prospective demographic trend or potential behavioral change may not, in itself, constitute a contingency or assumed risk that must be recognized, disclosed, or reported pursuant to SFFAS 5. Likewise, it may not be something that must be discussed in MD&A pursuant to the *Standards for Management's Discussion and Analysis* [SFFAS 15]. Even so, if there is a reasonable prospect of a major effect on the reporting entity due to the anticipated condition, then MD&A should include this information to the extent feasible.

35. Where appropriate, the description of possible future effects of both existing and anticipated factors should include quantitative forecasts or projections. Such forecasts or projections can show the implications of existing policies and conditions in light of anticipated or reasonably possible future conditions. For example, for MD&A of the Government-wide financial statements, long-term projections of the deficit or surplus may be important indicators of financial condition and sustainability. For insurance programs, this kind of projection—which actuaries sometimes call "dynamic analysis"—would consider possible interactions among current assets, reserves, policies in force, expected future business or populations covered by the insurance, and potential behavioral changes such as adverse selection and moral hazard, if appropriate. Some programs are inter-related among themselves and/or with conditions in the private sector. For example, flood insurance programs and disaster assistance programs may be related to such an extent that analysis of programs individually would not provide a good idea of their potential impact on the Government. To the extent feasible, projections should consider the potential implications of such relationships.

36. The future implications of current or anticipated factors often can better be expressed as a range of possible outcomes and associated probabilities than as a single point estimate. Sometimes the implications may best be discussed in nonfinancial as well as financial terms. Forward-looking information can be highly useful, but management should avoid turning this part of MD&A into mere "lobbying" for more budgetary authority.

Although it is considered a Primary Near-Term Focus Objective, the Stewardship Objective is considered a lower focus among the Primary Near-Term Focus Objectives (when compared to the Operating Performance Objective) because it has been addressed somewhat through existing FASAB requirements, is being addressed through other means and will be addressed as an integral part of meeting the Operating Performance Objective.

Also, considering that the Stewardship Objective addresses several sub-objectives that differ, one could rank the sub-objectives. This ranking would actually fall in line with the order presented in SFFAC 1 and included on page 4.) One could argue that the first sub-objective "the government's financial position improved or deteriorated over the period" could in essence be ranked as a higher priority among the Stewardship Objective sub-objectives. The first sub-objective involves assessing the government's financial position from one period to another, which is very important in analyzing operations and many aspects that could be considered similar to those of the Operating Performance Objective (and discussed in detail in the Operating Performance Objective Narrative on page 16). Therefore, this sub-objective would be considered the highest priority among the Stewardship sub-objectives.

FASAB's Secondary Near-Term Focus Objectives

Based on the assessment and consideration of the factors noted above, FASAB determined its Secondary Near-Term Focus Objectives are the Budgetary Integrity Objective and the Systems and Control Objective. A summary of the factors considered for placing these two objectives as Secondary near-term Focus Objectives is below.

Budgetary Integrity

Although the information that meets this objective is considered very important, the Budgetary Integrity Objective is considered a Secondary Near-Term Focus Objective because the Board's authority does not extend to budgetary measurement and recognition standards and therefore to a degree, limits the Board's comparative advantage in this area. The objective is also considered a Secondary Near-Term Focus Objective for the reasons discussed below—language from SFFAC 1, results from the roundtable meetings, other reports fulfilling this objective, and current FASAB standards and concepts statements.

Language from SFFAC 1 Regarding FASAB's Authority

The Board's authority does not extend to recommending budgetary standards or concepts. Specifically, par. 46 of SFFAC 1 states: "Although the FASAB does not recommend standards for the budget or budget concepts, part of its mission is to recommend accounting principles that will help provide relevant and reliable financial information to support the budgetary process. Furthermore, information about budget execution is essential to assessing budgetary integrity."

Rather, the Board has recognized that assurance regarding the reliability of budget information could be accomplished through financial reporting and subjecting the budgetary statements to audit. Specifically, SFFAC 1 paragraphs 190-191 state:

> 190. The Board's authority does not extend to recommending budgetary standards or budgetary concepts, but the Board is committed to providing reliable accounting information that supports budget planning and formulation. The Board also supports efforts to ensure the accuracy and reliability of reporting on the budget.

> 191. The Board's own focus is on developing generally accepted accounting standards for reporting on the financial operations, financial position, and financial condition of the federal government and its component entities and other useful financial information. This implies a variety of measures of costs and other information that complements the information available in the budget. Together with budgetary reports, these reports will provide a more comprehensive and insightful understanding of the government's financial position, results of operations, and financial condition than either set of reports alone.

Other Language from SFFAC 1

In addition, SFFAC 1 recognizes that accrual-based financial statements may not be the primary means of achieving the Budgetary Integrity Objective, and that the *Budget of the U.S. Government* is the main focus. Most would agree that the budget is the most widely recognized and used financial report of the federal government. The budget provides a system for controlling expenditures. SFFAC 1 par. 113 states "This objective arises generally from the responsibility of representative governments to be accountable for the monies that are raised and spent and for compliance with law.... Its focus is the Budget of the United States Government, the President's annual budget submission to the Congress, which is the government's principal financial report, and the laws enacting budget authority for a given fiscal year. The Budget of the United States Government is the initial frame of reference within which Congress and the President enact the laws that require the payment of taxes and provide the authority to obligate and spend money."

SFFAC 1 par. 121 further reiterates that budgetary measurements are used to address the Budgetary Integrity Objective by stating: "Reports primarily intended to address objective 1 and its first two sub-objectives would use budgetary measurement. Sub-objective 1C would use both budgetary and accrual measures because reconciliation of the two is implied..."

In addition, SFFAC 2 recognized that each reporting objective could be achieved through different reporting. Par. 56 of SFFAC 2 states "For example, the objective of budgetary integrity can be best met with the program and financing schedules prepared for individual budget accounts."

Roundtable Meetings

The participants at the Budgetary Integrity Roundtable agreed that financial reporting and the related audit have improved the reliability of budgetary data and information. The participants noted that there were some ways that the Budgetary information could be enhanced but recognized the fact that FASAB does not prescribe budgetary standards and determining how to align accounts and sub-accounts to programs may not be within FASAB's authority. The participants noted that there are other ways of meeting the needs of internal users and achieving the Budgetary Integrity Objective without FASAB involvement.

Based on the discussions of the roundtable participants, it appears that the Budgetary Integrity Objective would be considered a Secondary Near-Term Focus Objective for FASAB. A brief summary of each of the roundtable meetings is provided in Appendix V, Objectives Roundtable Meetings.

Other Reports Fulfilling this Objective

There are several other current reports that provide information to fulfill the Budgetary Integrity Objective. For example, as discussed above, the Budget of the United States Government is considered the government's principal financial report and provides much of the information necessary to meet the Budgetary Integrity Objective because it provides detailed budget information such as:

- The amount by account that each agency may obligate the Government to pay (budget authority) and estimates of payments (outlays) by agency and account;
- The amount of receipts each agency collects from various sources;
- Budget authority, outlays, and receipts by major function of Government, such as national defense;

- Total budget authority, outlays, and receipts for the Government; and
- The actual or estimated surplus (when receipts exceed outlays) or deficit (when outlays exceed receipts).[13]

Also, budget execution information is reported in the Report on Budget Execution and Budgetary Resources (SF 133). The SF 133 presents information that facilitates monitoring the status of budgetary resources and provides a consistent presentation of information across programs within each agency, and across agencies. Consistent presentation helps program, budget, and accounting staffs communicate. The report also provides a historical reference that can be used to help prepare the President's Budget and program operating plans. Other reports that contribute to the Budgetary Integrity Objective include CBO's Analysis of the President's Budget and the Budget and Economic Outlook Report.

Consideration of FASAB's Current Standards and Other Concepts Statements

In addition to other reports, FASAB concepts and standards have helped achieve the Budgetary Integrity Objective. SFFAC 2, SFFAS 7, *Accounting for Revenue and Other Financing Sources and Concepts for Reconciling Budgetary and Financial Accounting*, and the Implementation Guide to SFFAS 7 provide guidance related to reporting information to assist users of budgetary information. For instance, SFFAC 2 paragraphs 63 and 64 state:

63. Meeting the first objective of SFFAC No. 1, "Objectives of Federal Financial Reporting," namely the budgetary integrity objective, necessitates that the reader receive assurance that

- the amounts obligated or spent did not exceed the available budget authority,
- obligations and outlays were for the purposes intended in the appropriations and authorizing legislation,
- other legal requirements pertaining to the account have been met, and
- the amounts are properly classified and accurately reported.

64. This information is provided in other reports, but there needs to be auditor involvement to provide assurance as to the reliability of the information. The assurance as to reliability of the information could be accomplished by including a **statement of budgetary resources** in the reporting entity's financial statements, recognizing that the statement will likely be subject to audit. The presentation of data could be for the reporting entity as a whole, for the major suborganization units (assuming there is congruity among the major suborganization units and the budget

---

[13] OMB Circular A-11, par. 10.3.

accounts), or for the aggregations of the major budget accounts, rather than for the individual budget accounts of the entity or other types of entities. Violations of budgetary integrity at the account level occurring during the current year could be disclosed on an exception basis. (Many violations of budgetary integrity would also be violations of the Anti-Deficiency Act. Disclosure in the financial statements notwithstanding, these violations would also have to be reported as required by the Act.)

With the issuance of SFFAS 7, FASAB acknowledged that financial statements had not previously presented budget execution information needed by the users of budget execution reports.[14] SFFAS 7 presented standards to require the presentation and, consequently, the audit of information about budgetary resources, the status of those resources, and outlays. Also, SFFAS 7 required that the Statement of Financing explain how budgetary resources obligated during the period relate to the net cost of operations for that reporting entity. This information should be presented in a way that clarifies the relationship between the obligation basis of budgetary accounting and the accrual basis of financial (i.e., proprietary) accounting. The SFFAS 7 Implementation Guide provides detailed information about the Statement of Financing and explains its underlying concepts.

Therefore it would be appropriate for the Board to assess the Budgetary Integrity Objective as a Secondary Near-Term Focus Objective because it has been addressed somewhat through existing FASAB requirements, is being addressed through other means, and because the Board's authority does not extend to recommending budgetary standards or concepts. Nonetheless, as explained earlier, the Board believes that Secondary Near-Term Focus Objectives may be re-prioritized as fundamental issues are resolved in the long-term. Further, the Board believes that many of its active projects will address multiple objectives so that designation of a Secondary Near-Term Focus Objective does not preclude progress on meeting it. Further, it is possible that resources may become available to contribute to meeting this objective.

Systems and Control

Although the Systems and Control Objective remains a significant objective of federal financial reporting, it is considered a Secondary Near-Term Focus Objective for FASAB in the near-term. Its significance is evident in the many reforms and initiatives that have occurred in the past few years. The Systems and Control Objective is assessed lowest among FASAB's priorities because the Board plans to continue with an indirect approach toward achieving this objective in the near-term.

---

[14] SFFAS 7, Summary.

The objective's broad nature permits accounting standards and other sources to act and provide guidance. This flexibility appears to be working as intended. The OMB recently issued more rigorous internal control reporting requirements in the revised OMB Circular A-123, *Management's Responsibility for Internal Control,* and the requirements assist users in understanding the adequacy of systems and control. Considering that the requirements have yet to be fully implemented and the actual impact is not certain at this time, the Board's focus on this objective should be considered low while monitoring the agencies' progress.

Assessing the Systems and Control Objective as a Secondary Near-Term Focus Objective for FASAB and perhaps the lowest priority in relation to all of the objectives is based on the fact that the Board will continue to utilize an indirect approach to addressing the objective in the near-term and for the reasons discussed below— language from SFFAC 1, changes in environment due to new laws and administrative directives, results from the roundtable meetings, other reports fulfilling this objective, and current FASAB standards and concepts statements.

Indirect Approach and Language from SFFAC 1

Most would agree that FASAB standards have had an "indirect" impact on achieving the Systems and Control Objective. For example, the ability to prepare financial statements could be considered as an indication that essential internal controls exist; therefore, information on systems and control is a by-product of the federal accounting standards. Further support for this indirect approach to achieving the Systems and Control Objective can be found in the SFFAC 1 discussion relating to the objective. Specifically, par. 147-149 of SFFAC 1 describes the Systems and Control Objective as follows:

147. This objective arises from the three preceding objectives, in conjunction with the fact that accounting supports both effective management and control of organizations and the process of reporting useful information. Indeed, accounting processes are an integral part of the management control system.

148. The ability to prepare financial reports that report all transactions, classified in appropriate ways that faithfully represent the underlying events, is itself an indication that certain essential controls are in place and operating effectively. The preparation of reliable financial reports also helps to ensure that reporting entities have early warning systems to indicate potential problems and take actions to correct material weaknesses or problems.

149. Sound controls over internal processes are essential both to safeguard assets and to ensure economy, efficiency, and effectiveness in many governmental programs.

There is a discussion in the Basis for Conclusions that demonstrates respondents (to the SFFAC 1 exposure draft) also believed that the Systems and Control Objective is accomplished through the other objectives, as par. 237 of SFFAC 1 includes the following: "Others suggested that a separate objective on this topic was not necessary because it could be inferred from the other objectives." However, the Board explained the following view in response to the above in par. 238 of SFFAC 1: "With regard to the fundamental point, however, the Board continues to believe that systems and control are topics of sufficient importance and relevance to warrant addressing in their own right."

Changes in the Environment due to Laws and Administrative Directives

Further support for the lower priority of the Systems and Control Objective is provided when one considers the evolution of federal financial reporting laws and administrative directives. As mentioned earlier in this document, since the CFO Act, Congress has enacted a series of laws to report on and improve financial management in the federal government. It was noted that there were several new laws and administrative directives related to internal control (such as FFMIA, SOX, and OMB Circular A-123) that focused on informing users about agency systems of accounting, financial management, and internal controls. In particular, the revised OMB Circular A-123 requires management assurance statements on internal control, including a separate assurance on internal control over financial reporting. The legislation and administrative directives noted in this area focused on the improvement of agency systems of accounting, financial management, and internal controls. It appears that most of the legislation and administrative directives in this area have a direct relationship with the Systems and Control Objective. Agency efforts to comply with the legislation and administrative directives in this area (and the resulting oversight by OMB) seem to significantly contribute to meeting certain aspects of the Systems and Control Objective. The extent to which this objective is addressed through other means impacts the assessment of FASAB's focus on this particular objective. Considering the requirements have yet to be fully implemented and the actual impact is not certain at this time, the Board's focus on this objective should be considered low while monitoring the agencies' progress. Accordingly, GAAP standards promulgated by FASAB to meet the Systems and Control Objective do not appear to be a high priority at this time.

A detailed summary and analysis of the impact of each pertinent law and administrative directive is presented in Appendix IV, *Evolutions in Federal Financial Management and Reporting Laws and Administrative Directives since the CFO Act of 1990*.

Roundtable Meetings

The participants at the Systems and Control Roundtable believed that the Systems and Control Objective remains valid in today's environment and agreed with the indirect role of standards in achieving the objective. The participants did not convey a need for changes to the Systems and Control Objective. Instead, they discussed the importance of the objective in federal financial reporting, and they discussed methods that could enhance achievement of the objective.

The participants did not believe that FASAB should issue a specific standard on systems and control. Most of the participants expressed support for FASAB to continue the indirect approach as it related to systems and control. In addition, the participants explained that an indirect approach rather than prescriptive guidelines enables the Board to be encompassing for everyone to accomplish their mission.

The participants did not identify a need for FASAB to engage in setting standards concerning internal control. Some saw this as the Government Accountability Office's (GAO) role and it was noted that on December 21, 2004, the Office of Management and Budget (OMB) issued a revised OMB Circular A-123. OMB Circular A-123 requires a management assurance statement on the effectiveness of internal control over financial reporting. Rather than issuing a standard, it was expressed that perhaps FASAB could refer to OMB Circular A-123 and state that the Board endorses the notion of management's reporting on controls over financial reporting.

Certain participants offered that FASAB, with its limited resources, should focus on addressing the direct technical accounting issues that remain. The participants believed the projects on FASAB's current technical agenda as well as those that are often the subject of inquiries are more important when compared to areas related to systems and control.

Based on the discussions of the roundtable participants, the Systems and Control Objective would be considered a Secondary Near-Term Focus Objective for FASAB. A brief summary of each of the roundtable meetings is provided in Appendix V, Objectives Roundtable Meetings.

Other Reports Fulfilling this Objective

There are several other current reports that provide information to fulfill the Systems and Control Objective. The FMFIA requires GAO to prescribe standards of internal accounting and administrative control and agencies to comply with them. It also requires OMB to establish guidelines for agency evaluation of internal control to determine compliance with the internal control standards and agency heads are required to (1) annually evaluate their internal control using the OMB guidelines, and (2) annually report to the President on whether the agency's internal controls comply with the standards and objectives set forth in the Act.

In addition to the FMFIA, the FFMIA[15] requires CFO Act agencies to implement and maintain financial management systems that can comply substantially with system requirements, applicable federal accounting standards, and the Standard General Ledger. The FFMIA also requires that the agency annual audit report state whether the agency's financial management systems comply with the requirements.

Agencies include information on internal control in their PARs. OMB Circular A-123 requires management assurance statements on internal control, including the effectiveness of internal control over financial reporting, and OMB Circular A-136 requires agencies to include the assurance statements in the MD&A section of the PAR. Also, generally accepted government auditing standards require auditors to report on the scope of their testing of internal control over financial reporting and of compliance with laws and regulations. Agencies include the auditor's reports in the PAR.

In addition, the internal control weaknesses identified through the assessment and audit processes are monitored regularly. As part of the PMA, OMB monitors internal control weaknesses and agencies must eliminate all internal control weaknesses to receive green on the PMA scorecard. Agencies submit corrective action plans to OMB to resolve internal control weaknesses reported and OMB grades the agencies on their progress in achieving the corrective action milestones contained in their plans.

---

[15] Unlike FMFIA, which generally applies to executive branch agencies, FFMIA applies only to the executive branch agencies that are subject to the CFO Act.

Consideration of FASAB's Current Standards and Other Concepts Statements

Within the stated objective, FASAB concepts and standards have contributed to ensuring that federal entities report on internal control. In addition to the many accounting standards that indirectly contributed to the objective, the concepts and standards for MD&A in the financial statements have had a direct impact.

SFFAC 3 discusses the significance of the Systems and Control Objective and the relationship between a federal entity's internal controls and its financial statements. The Board noted that reporting information that helps people understand the condition of the entity's internal control is an important objective of federal financial reporting. The Board also noted that financial statements alone do not provide adequate information about the status of the entity's internal control that support reporting on financial and operating performance and reporting on compliance with applicable laws. Consequently, SFFAC 3 provided that in addition to its basic financial statements, a federal entity should include information about internal control and legal compliance.

The Board then developed standards for MD&A that would include requirements for internal control. In SFFAS 15, the Board stated that each general purpose federal financial report should include an MD&A section. SFFAS 15 provides that the MD&A is regarded as required supplementary information and it should include information on the federal entity's internal control. The Board suggested that OMB might provide more prescriptive guidance by stating: "More specific requirements regarding the content of MD&A may be added later by OMB acting on its own authority or pursuant to future FASAB recommendations."

With the MD&A being an integral part of the entity's financial report and providing the link between information on internal control and the financial statements, the OMB acted and provided more prescriptive guidance. The revised OMB Circular A-123 requires management assurance statements on internal control, including a separate assurance on internal control over financial reporting.

Therefore it would be appropriate for the Board to assess the Systems and Control Objective as a Secondary Near-Term Focus Objective because the reporting of information on systems and control has been addressed somewhat through existing FASAB requirements, is being addressed through other means, and because the Board plans to continue with an indirect approach in achieving this objective in the near-term. Information on internal control is a by-product of the federal accounting standards and, therefore, most active projects would naturally result in achievement of some aspects of this objective. In addition, as explained earlier, the Board believes that Secondary Near-Term Focus Objectives may be re-prioritized as fundamental issues are resolved in the long-term. Further, it is possible that resources may become available to contribute to meeting this objective.

Conclusion on FASAB's Strategic Directions

By providing FASAB's Strategic Directions, the Board clarifies its near-tem role in achieving the broad objectives of financial reporting. Defining FASAB's role in meeting each objective was not a ranking of the broad objectives. Instead, it was an assessment of which objectives there would be more opportunity to play a direct role in achieving through accounting standards developed in the near-term.

FASAB's assessment of the objectives provided that there are two types of focus for FASAB in the near-term. Primary Near-Term Focus Objectives are objectives where there is the greatest opportunity for FASAB to play a direct role by developing standards to achieve the stated objectives. FASAB determined its Primary Near-Term Focus Objectives are the Operating Performance Objective and the Stewardship Objective. Secondary Near-Term Focus Objectives are objectives where there is not the greatest opportunity for FASAB to play a direct role by developing standards to achieve the stated objectives. In contrast to Primary Near-Term Focus Objectives, FASAB believes that for the most part it will play a supporting role in meeting these objectives in the near-term. FASAB determined its Secondary Near-Term Focus Objectives are the Budgetary Integrity Objective and the Systems and Control Objective.

The Board believes that Secondary Near-Term Focus Objectives may be re-prioritized as fundamental issues are resolved in the long-term. In the near-term, the Board believes that many of its active projects will address multiple objectives so that designation of a "secondary near-term focus" or "supporting role" objective does not preclude progress on meeting those objectives.

Also, to implement the overall guidance provided by the strategic directions, the Board will continue to consider the following criteria[16] in evaluating specific projects for its technical agenda:

1. Significance of the issue relative to meeting reporting objectives;
2. Pervasiveness of the issue among federal entities; and,
3. Technical outlook and resource needs.

As stated, FASAB may re-evaluate this assessment periodically in conjunction with other strategic planning efforts.

---

[16] Appendix I, *Criteria for Ranking Projects* provides additional information on each of these factors.

APPENDIX I – Criteria for Ranking Projects

Adopted by FASAB on October 21, 2004

1. **Significance of the issue relative to meeting reporting objectives**
   a. With respect to meeting reporting objectives, are one or more alternative solutions likely to produce an improvement in information that is important to external, legislative, and executive branch users?
   b. Is the issue so egregious that not resolving it would damage the credibility of federal financial reporting?
   c. Is current practice diverse among federal entities and is comparability between federal entities important in this area?
   d. Is financial information that is relevant, reliable and comparable already available and likely to remain available?
   e. Is it likely that the project will clarify the federal reporting model or lead to concepts that provide a sound foundation for future projects?

2. **Pervasiveness of the issue among federal entities**
   a. Are many federal entities faced with this issue?
   b. Are significant dollar effects on federal financial reports likely?
   c. Is the issue raised by a single event unlikely to recur often and/or for which level A GAAP guidance could not be provided in a timely manner (e.g., major restructuring of departments)?
   d. Is there existing ambiguity, which contributes to divergence of practice or other difficulties for preparers, auditors and users?

3. **Technical outlook and resource needs**
   a. Have other standard setters done research or developed a standard(s) that could be useful to FASAB?
   b. Are other standard setters currently undertaking projects of potential significance to federal accounting such that a simultaneous project would be desirable?
   c. Are there sufficient resources available to research and resolve the question on a timely basis?
      i. Would a task force of preparers, auditors and/or users be needed and available to assist?
      ii. Are Board resources balanced appropriately between major projects and projects that offer technical guidance or fill voids in applying existing standards?
   d. Are there barriers to finding a solution that is likely to be accepted generally? (e.g., Would legislation be required to compel compliance? Would extensive changes to systems or the audit model be needed to successfully address the issue?)

APPENDIX II--Evolution in FASAB

FASAB Created

In October 1990, the Secretary of the Treasury, the Director of the Office of Management and Budget, and the Comptroller General of the United States established the Federal Accounting Standards Advisory Board (FASAB or "the Board") as a federal advisory committee.

The nine member FASAB consisted of representatives from the three principles, one Congressional Budget Office representative, one representative from the defense and international agencies, one representative from civilian agencies, and three representatives from the private sector. FASAB issued recommended statements of accounting concepts and standards for approval by its three principals. In developing the statements, the FASAB adhered to Federal Advisory Committee Act requirements and engaged a seven-step due process approach that included public participation.

1. Identification of accounting issues and agenda decisions.
2. Preliminary deliberations.
3. Preparation of initial documents (issue papers, and/or discussion memorandums).
4. Release of documents (e.g., exposure drafts) to the public, public hearings, and consideration of comments.
5. Further deliberations and consideration of comments.
6. General consensus (at least a majority vote) reached among Board members and final documents submitted to the Treasury, OMB, and GAO for approval.
7. The Principals provide for implementation guidance through the FASAB's Accounting and Auditing Policy Committee.

Shortly after FASAB was established, the Chief Financial Officers Act of 1990 became law. The Act established the position of Chief Financial Officer in each department and selected executive agencies to ensure the development of integrated agency accounting and financial management systems, including financial reporting and internal controls, which comply with applicable accounting principles, standards, and requirements, and internal control standards. The CFO Act also required some executive agencies to have agency-wide audited financial statements and other agencies to have more limited statements. The Government Management Reform Act of 1994 for the first time required annual audited financial statements covering the entire executive branch as well as agency-wide statements for each agency covered by the CFO Act.

GAAP Status Attained

In October 1999, the American Institute of Certified Public Accountants' (AICPA) Council designated the FASAB as the accounting standards-setting body for federal government entities under Rule 203 of the AICPA's Code of Professional Conduct. Rule 203 provides, in part, that an AICPA member shall not (1) express an opinion or state affirmatively that the financial statements or other financial data of any entity are presented in conformity with generally accepted accounting principles (GAAP) or (2) state that he or she is not aware of any material modifications that should be made to such statements or data in order for them to be in conformity with GAAP, if such statements or data contain any departure from an accounting principle promulgated by bodies designated by Council to establish such principles, that has a material effect on the statements or data taken as a whole.

Until the AICPA action, the federal government did not have a Rule 203 designated accounting standards-setter.[17] With this designation, federal government reporting entities obtain audit opinions that indicate that the financial statements are presented in conformity with GAAP rather than an "other comprehensive basis of accounting" (OCBOA).

This designation came after an AICPA task force evaluated FASAB against the following criteria used in designating accounting standards-setting bodies under Rule 203: Independence; Due Process and Standards; Domain and Authority; Human and Financial Resources; and Comprehensiveness and Consistency.

The task force recommended some enhancements in FASAB's procedures, and assisted in incorporating them in FASAB's Memorandum of Understanding and Rules of Procedure. The most significant enhancements were:

- creation of an Appointments Panel to assist in selecting non-federal members;
- opening Steering Committee meetings to the public; and
- establishing that FASAB would issue final standards following a review period.

With the enhancements completed, the task force deemed the FASAB to have satisfied such criteria. Accordingly, the AICPA Board recommended that the Council adopt a

---

[17] The AICPA Council designated the Financial Accounting Standards Board (FASB) as the standards-setter for the private sector in 1973 and the Governmental Accounting Standards Board (GASB) as the standards-setter for state and local governments in 1986. These are authoritative standard-setting bodies under Rule 203.

resolution to designate FASAB under Rule 203 for an initial five year period. On October 19, 1999, the AICPA Council approved the resolution.[18]

Subsequent to the Rule 203 recognition, the FASAB changed how it issued accounting concepts and standards. Previously, standards developed by FASAB did not become final until the sponsors explicitly approved them for issuance. With the change, FASAB forwards standards to the sponsors for a 90-day review. FASAB also forwards capital asset accounting standards to the Congress for the mandatory 45-day review. If there are no objections during these respective review periods, the standards are considered final and FASAB publishes them on its website.

Additional enhancements following the October 1999 AICPA recognition of FASAB as the standard-setting body for the federal government are reflected in its operating documents. These enhancements included the following:

- Minutes are posted to the FASAB website after each Board meeting (see http://www.fasab.gov/meeting.htm);
- Briefing materials (except for draft Board issuances) are available in advance of each Board meeting via the FASAB website (see http://www.fasab.gov/meeting.htm);
- Procedures for issuing Technical Bulletins were established;
- Exposure drafts are published electronically and hard copies are available on request;
- Any dissents and the identify of the authors are published in final statements;
- Press releases have been improved and a broader list of press contacts is maintained; and,
- Agenda setting process now includes a call for comments on proposed projects and permits identification of other project proposals.

Enhancements to Independence

In 2002, the Board's sponsors altered the Board's structure to increase the level of non-federal representation to enhance the perceived independence of the Board. The nine-member board would now have six non-federal members and three federal members. In addition, the Secretary of the Treasury relinquished his authority to object to any standard during the 90-day review period. Thus, only GAO and OMB may object to the issuance of a new standard or concept by FASAB.

---

[18] On May 23, 2003 the AICPA Council unanimously voted to continue for a second five-year period designation of the FASAB as the accounting standards-setting body for Federal government entities under Rule 203 of the AICPA's Code of Professional Conduct.

In 2003, the Board was expanded to provide for additional legislative branch input. The Board grew to ten members with the addition of a representative from the Congressional Budget Office. The Board now has six non-federal members and four federal members.

Other Board Activities

The FASAB engages in several activities to accomplish its mission. Those activities include:

- Determining the primary users of federal financial information and their needs;

- Developing accounting standards and principles that improve the usefulness of financial reports based on the needs of users and on the primary characteristics of understandability, relevance, and reliability;

- Providing advice to central financial agencies on implementing the standards;

- Improving the common understanding of information contained in financial reports;

- Developing standards and principles that take into account expected benefits and perceived costs;

- Reviewing the effects of current standards and develop amendments or new standards when appropriate;

- Using a thoughtful, open, neutral, and fair deliberative process and consider the accountability and decision-making needs of users;

- Developing rules of procedures designed to permit timely, thorough, and open study of financial accounting and reporting issues and to encourage broad public participation in all phases of the accounting standard-setting process; and,

- Being objective and neutral and ensure, as much as possible, that the information resulting from its proposed standards is a faithful representation of the effects of federal government activities. Objective and neutral means free from bias, precluding the FASAB from placing any particular interest above the interests of the many who rely on the information contained in financial reports.[19]

In addition, the Board observes the activities of other accounting standards-setting authorities and seeks their views on proposed concepts and standards. For instance, as part of the Board's definition and recognition of elements project, the Board provided the IPSASB with an exposure draft of the proposed concepts statement and staff reviewed IPSASB literature for materials that may be related to the FASAB project.

---

[19] FASAB Facts 2006.

APPENDIX III--GAAP AND NON-GAAP REPORTING

For FASAB's purposes, financial reporting comprises GAAP reporting and non-GAAP reporting.

GAAP Reporting

Reports prepared in accordance with GAAP are designed to convey a *fair presentation* of an entity's financial position, results of operations, financing of operations and certain projections critical to meeting reporting objectives. GAAP reports have three components:

1. *Principal financial statements.* Principal financial statements recognize elements --broad classes of items, such as assets, liabilities, revenues, and expenses, that comprise the building blocks of financial statements. The Balance Sheet, Statement of Net Cost, and Statement of Changes in Net Position that are derived from the process of accrual accounting articulate with one another and present elements recognized in monetary units. Non-accrual financial statements such as the Statements of Budgetary Resources and Social Insurance also present elements recognized in monetary units. These statements provide a consistent and disciplined presentation of budgetary resources as well as certain critical financial projections related to financial condition.

2. *Notes to financial statements.* Note disclosures generally are considered an integral part of financial statements, but they are not elements. They serve different functions, including amplifying or complementing information about items reported in the body of financial statements. For example, integral note disclosures explain and amplify the elements recognized in the financial statements and any unrecognized elements and specific contingencies with potential impact on future recognition or measurement of financial statement elements.

3. *Supplemental disclosures.* Supplemental disclosures, such as the MD&A, explain significant period to period changes in the elements reported in the financial statements. Supplemental disclosures may provide information on internal and external matters that are relevant to an understanding of present and future financial position and results of operations.

The federal financial reporting model includes both accrual and non-accrual based financial statements. Accrual accounting starts with raw cash flows and varies the timing of their recognition to coincide with the events that cause the cash flows. Also, accrual accounting is concerned with measuring costs and revenues for a period and measuring asset and liability positions at the beginning and end of the period and analyzing the reasons for change from one period to another. It offers benefits such as:

- *Prediction and Feedback.* Accrual accounting informs an entity where it stands financially at the end of each period. Knowledge of the current position provides a starting point for planning and predicting future actions.

- *Disciplined GAAP Framework.* Accrual accounting leads to an independently testable discipline in the measurement process and all of an entity's existing assets and liabilities can be assessed in relation to one another and to aggregates and to changes over time. It also assists in reporting on accountability and decision making.

Non-GAAP Reporting

Non-GAAP Reporting includes all reporting of financial information except for GAAP reporting. It includes out-year budgetary information and projections as well as analyses of historical information. It ranges from a concentration on minute details to presentation of global perspectives.

Audit

Under the AICPA's ethics rules, no CPA may assert that a federal entity's financial statements **fairly present** financial position and results of operations in accordance with GAAP unless the information presented conforms to FASAB standards in all material respects. If agencies are directed to prepare financial reports consistent with GAAP and subject them to audit, FASAB standards govern the preparation and are the benchmark against which auditors provide assurance. In setting the accounting standards, FASAB determines the extent of audit by specifying in accounting standards whether required financial information is **basic** or **supplemental.**

Basic information refers to the first two components of GAAP reports – elements recognized in the principal financial statements and integral note disclosures. Auditors of federal entities conduct audits of basic information in accordance with Generally

Accepted Government Auditing Standards (GAGAS). GAGAS incorporates auditing standards issued by the AICPA.

Supplemental information is the third component of GAAP reports. GAGAS incorporates the AICPA audit procedures to be followed for supplemental information. The audit requirements are typically less intensive than requirements for basic information.

Non-GAAP reports may be audited for special purposes as determined by the preparer entity and user entities, but there is no general requirement that they be audited and usually they are not.

FASAB's Role Concerning GAAP Reporting

Under its designation by the profession as the Rule 203 standard setter, FASAB has exclusive jurisdiction for determining what information is essential for *fair presentation* and for formulating concepts and standards for GAAP reporting by federal entities. FASAB standards are the core of federal GAAP. Some GAAP is a result of long-standing accounting practice that is not formally mandated but is required to be followed for purposes of rendering opinions under GAGAS. FASAB can override this informal kind of GAAP by issuing standards.

FASAB's Role Concerning Non-GAAP Reporting

FASAB may develop standards regarding specific non-GAAP information to be reported for experimental purposes with a view to incorporating it in GAAP reports if the information proves to be useful. FASAB may also encourage, promote, or assist in the development of the reporting of specific non-GAAP information as part of joint efforts with its sponsoring organizations for purposes of improving overall federal financial reporting. For the most part, however, non-GAAP reporting is undertaken by federal entities on their own initiative or under direction from OMB, the Congress, or others.

APPENDIX IV--Evolution in Federal Financial Management and Reporting Laws and Administrative Directives since the CFO Act of 1990

The CFO Act could be considered the first of a series of major legislation passed beginning in 1990 to improve federal accountability through financial management reform. Briefly, the purposes of the CFO Act were to (1) bring more effective financial management practices to the federal government, (2) provide for the production of complete, reliable, and consistent financial information for use in management and evaluation of federal programs, and (3) improve agency systems of accounting, financial management, and internal controls. The CFO Act created 24 chief financial officers for the major executive departments and agencies. In addition to requiring those agencies to prepare and submit audited financial statements for each revolving and trust fund and for accounts that performed substantial commercial functions, the CFO Act required some agencies to have agency-wide financial statements.

Since then, and following in the steps of the CFO Act, Congress has enacted a series of laws to reform and improve financial management in the federal government. Along the lines of the three purposes of the CFO Act described in the previous paragraph, the legislation and administrative directives since 1993 broadly fall into the three areas:

- **Effective Financial Management Practices**--Legislation and administrative directives to bring more effective financial management practices to the federal government;
- **Performance Measurement**--Legislation and administrative directives to provide for the production of complete, reliable, and consistent financial information for use in management and evaluation of federal programs; and
- **Internal Controls**--Legislation and administrative directives to improve agency systems of accounting, financial management, and internal controls.

Accordingly, it would be appropriate to consider these and the related changes in the federal financial reporting environment since SFFAC 1 was issued in 1993. A brief summary and analysis of implications for pertinent laws and administrative directives is presented below.

Effective Financial Management Practices

Government Management Reform Act of 1994 (GMRA)--GMRA substantially expanded the requirements in the CFO Act by requiring audited financial statements covering all accounts in the 24 CFO agencies. In addition, GMRA also required the Secretary of the

Treasury to prepare a consolidated financial statement for the executive branch. From its inception, the resulting Financial Report of the United States Government has also included financial information for the legislative and judicial branches.

Impact/Analysis: During FASAB's early years, it focused more on financial statements for components or segments of the federal government than it did on the government-wide statements. It was understood that some differences would be appropriate at the government-wide level (e.g., with regard to reporting on budgetary execution and financing). It was expected that—in the absence of specific guidance from FASAB—OMB, GAO and Treasury would determine how to report at the government-wide level. GMRA's requirement for audited financial statements at this level and AICPA's recognition of federal accounting principles published by FASAB as GAAP (in SAS 91, *Federal GAAP Hierarchy*, April 2000), created a need for FASAB to define the applicable standards and to consider whether additional or different concepts were needed. FASAB has done so in SFFAC 4, *Intended Audience and Qualitative Characteristics for the Consolidated Financial Report of the United States Government*, and in SFFAS 24, *Selected Standards for the Consolidated Financial Report of the United Statements Government*. In addition, FASAB now includes a separate section detailing requirements for the Government-wide financial statement in applicable standards.

Reports Consolidation Act of 2000--This Reports Consolidation Act builds on a pilot program authorized in GMRA that allowed an agency to combine its audited financial statement, as required by GMRA, and its performance reports, as required by GPRA, to provide a more comprehensive and useful picture of the services provided. The 2000 Act also identifies other management reports eligible for consolidation.

The Reports Consolidation Act requires that a consolidated report:

- Shall be referred to as a *Performance and Accountability Report* if it incorporates the agency's GPRA program performance report;
- Contain a summary of the most significant portions of the agency's program performance report, including the agency's success in achieving key performance goals, if the GPRA program performance report is not incorporated;
- Include a statement by the agency's inspector general that summarizes the agency's most serious management and performance challenges; and
- Include a transmittal letter from the agency head containing an assessment of the completeness and reliability of the performance and financial data used in the report.

Impact/Analysis: With the Reports Consolidation Act, agency audited financial statements are included in a combined Performance and Accountability Report that contain other financial and performance reporting requirements.

Accountability of Tax Dollars Act of 2002--The Accountability of Tax Dollars Act extended the requirements for preparation of audited financial statements to virtually all executive branch agencies. In addition, OMB has required these agencies to include a program performance report with their audited financial statements. OMB may exempt agencies with available budget authority under $25 million in a given year, if OMB determines that audited financial statements are not warranted due to an absence of risk. The agencies are subject to OMB Circular A-136, *Financial Reporting Requirements.* (Note that FFMIA reporting requirements were not applied to these newly covered agencies.)

Impact/Analysis: The Accountability of Tax Dollars Act extends the requirement to produce and audit financial statements to some relatively small federal entities.

Improper Payments Information Act of 2002--The Improper Payments Information Act requires federal agencies to identify programs vulnerable to improper payments and to estimate annually the amount of underpayments and overpayments made by these programs. OMB has directed agencies to report this information in the MD&A section of the Performance and Accountability Report.[20]

Impact/Analysis: Some may believe that this law suggests a need for FASAB to focus on this topic, much as FASAB focused on accounting for direct loans and loan guarantees after the Credit Reform Act was passed, and as FASAB focused on government-wide reporting after GMRA was passed. Others may believe that existing standards adequately address this topic, and/or that OMB action in this area and related guidance is sufficient.

---

[20] "Agencies shall include the reporting requirements of this guidance in the Management Discussion and Analysis section of their Performance and Accountability Report for fiscal years ending on or after September 30, 2004. The annual estimate of erroneous payments reported in the Performance and Accountability Report can be based on data from a year other than the fiscal year the Performance and Accountability Report covers. Progress under the requirements of Section 57 of OMB Circular A-11 shall be reported in the FY 2003 Performance and Accountability Reports." OMB Memorandum M-03-13, *Improper Payments Information Act of 2002 (Public Law No: 107-300),* issued May 21, 2003.

President's Management Agenda (PMA)--*Improved Financial Performance Initiative*--In addition to the above legislation and administrative directives, the President's Management Agenda represents an ongoing effort in the executive branch for improving management and performance in the federal government. The PMA, announced in the summer of 2001, is an aggressive strategy for improving the management of the federal government. It focuses on five areas of management weakness across the government where improvements and the most progress can be made.

Improved Financial Performance is one of the five government-wide initiatives. The financial management initiative seeks to enhance the quality and timeliness of financial information. This initiative also focuses on improving assets management and reducing improper payments.

A "Management Scorecard" is used to measure progress on the Agenda initiatives. The scorecard uses a traffic light system for rating agencies--green for success, yellow for mixed success, and red for unsatisfactory. For each initiative, there are core criteria that the agency must meet in order to get a green rating. OMB updates the scorecard on a quarterly basis.

The core criteria for "getting to green" on the improving financial performance initiative are:
- Financial management systems meet federal financial management system requirements and applicable federal accounting and transaction standards as reported by the agency head;
- Accurate and timely financial information;
- Integrated financial and performance management systems supporting day-today operations; and,
- Unqualified and timely audit opinions on the annual financial statements and no material internal control weaknesses.

A basic tenet of the PMA calls for improving financial performance by providing timely, reliable, and useful information. As a result, OMB amended OMB Bulletin 01-09 *Form and Content of Agency Financial Statements* to significantly accelerate financial reporting due dates. Specifically, beginning with fiscal year (FY) 2004, Performance and Accountability Reports were due to the President, OMB, and the Congress by November 15th. Additionally, Treasury was required to issue the Financial Report of the United States Government to the President and the Congress by December 15th. In addition, beginning with the quarter ending March 31, 2004, agencies were required to prepare and submit to OMB its quarterly unaudited financial statements 21 days after the end of each quarter. OMB recently issued Circular A-136, *Financial Reporting Requirements*, which replaces OMB Bulletin 01-09 and reiterates and incorporates the accelerated financial reporting and form and content requirements.

Impact/Analysis: The PMA has resulted in more timely financial reports and additional oversight by OMB and other agency initiatives to address these important areas related to improving financial performance.

Conclusion on Effective Financial Management Practices Legislation and Administrative Directives and Linkage to Objectives

Some legislation and administrative directives in this area focused on extending requirements of the CFO Act for audited financial statements from the original CFO agencies to other agencies as well as the consolidated government-wide financial statements. Legislation and administrative directives also focused on streamlining reporting requirements by allowing agencies to produce a Performance and Accountability Report. Additionally, agencies are issuing more timely financial reports due to the accelerated due dates. Agency efforts to comply with the legislation and administrative directives in this area have brought about more effective financial management practices, but do not appear to significantly contribute to meeting any one objective that would impact the assessment of FASAB's focus.

Performance Measurement

Government Performance and Results Act of 1993 (GPRA)--Briefly, the purposes of the GPRA include:
      (1) improved management of federal programs;
      (2) increased accountability and better assessment of results;
      (3) improved communication with Congress and the public;
      (4) better information for Congressional and agency decisions, and,
      (5) increased public confidence in the government.

GPRA requires agencies to prepare strategic plans, annual performance plans, and annual performance reports. The annual performance report examines whether goals (as discussed in the annual performance plan) were met and what was accomplished with the resources expended. It should be noted that agencies are required to consolidate their audited financial statements and other financial and performance reports into combined Performance and Accountability Reports.

Impact/Analysis: SFFAC 1 includes "Operating Performance" as one of the four objectives of federal financial reporting. Also, chapter 8 discusses "How Financial Reporting Supports Reporting on Operating Performance." Some may believe that these references to performance are sufficient and that no change is needed as a result of GPRA, but others may believe that an amplification of these sections of SFFAC 1 would be in order now that GPRA has led to performance reporting on a comprehensive basis while the Reports Consolidation Act have led agencies to include performance information with the audited financial statements in Performance and Accountability Reports.

However, other people may believe that no amplification of the concepts is needed, but that one or more statements of standards may be needed to address performance reporting. Some people may believe that provisions of existing concepts and standards issued by FASAB, such as SFFAC 3, *Management's Discussion and Analysis,* SFFAS 4, *Managerial Cost Accounting Concepts and Standards for the Federal Government,* and SFFAS 7, *Accounting for Revenue and Other Financing Sources*, SFFAS 15, *Management's Discussion and Analysis*, and SFFAS 30, *Inter-Entity Cost Implementation* adequately respond to these laws. Alternatively, other people may believe that OMB action pursuant to GPRA have effectively ended any need for FASAB to act in this area.

President's Management Agenda (PMA)--*Budget and Performance Integration Initiative-* In addition to GPRA, the PMA represents an ongoing effort in the executive branch for improving management and performance in the federal government. As stated above, the PMA, announced in the summer of 2001, is an aggressive strategy for improving the management of the federal government. It focuses on five areas of management weakness across the government where improvements and the most progress can be made.

Another initiative under the PMA is Budget and Performance Integration. The Budget and Performance Integration initiative seeks to formally integrate performance review with Budget decisions. A "Management Scorecard" is used to measure progress on the Agenda initiatives. The scorecard uses a traffic light system for rating agencies--green for success, yellow for mixed success, and red for unsatisfactory. For each initiative, there are core criteria that the agency must meet in order to get a green rating. OMB updates the scorecard on a quarterly basis.

The core criteria for "getting to green" on this initiative include: agency demonstrates improvement in program performance and efficiency in achieving results; annual budget and performance documents incorporate measures identified in the PART; agency reports the full cost of achieving performance goals accurately in budget and performance documents and can accurately estimate the marginal cost (+/- 10%) of changing performance goals; has at least one efficiency measure for all PART programs; and uses PART evaluations to direct program improvements, and PART ratings and performance information are used consistently to justify funding requests, management actions, and legislative proposals.

Impact/Analysis: The PMA has resulted in additional oversight by OMB and other agency initiatives to address these important areas related to budget and performance integration and full costing. See discussion under GPRA above for additional discussion.

OMB's Program Assessment Rating Tool (PART) Analysis--The Administration began (in the 2004 Budget) to assess federal programs by a method known as the PART. The primary purpose of the PART is to improve program performance in the federal government and is a key tool in the budget and performance integration initiative mentioned above.

The Administration set a target of assessing all federal programs over five years. The PART system assesses each program in four components--purpose, planning, management, and results/accountability--and gives a score for each of the components. The scores for each component are weighted and the program is given an overall score. A program is rated effective if it receives an overall score of 85 percent or more, moderately effective if the score is 70 to 84 percent, adequate if the score is 50 to 69 percent, and inadequate if the score is 49 percent or lower. The program receives a rating "Results Not Demonstrated" if it does not have a good long-term and annual performance measure or does not have data to report on its measures.

Impact/Analysis: The PART Analysis has resulted in additional oversight by OMB and other agency initiatives in the area of agency performance measurement and accountability. See additional discussion under GPRA above.

Conclusion on Performance Measurement Legislation and Administrative Directives and Linkage to Objectives

The legislation and administrative directives noted in this area focused on the production of complete and reliable performance information for use in management and evaluation of federal programs. It appears that most of the legislation and administrative directives in this area have a direct relationship with the Operating Performance Objective. In particular, they relate to this sub-objective: 'The efforts and accomplishments associated with federal programs and the changes over time and in relation to costs.' Agency efforts to comply with the legislation and administrative directives in this area (and the resulting oversight by OMB) seem to significantly contribute to meeting this sub-objective related to performance measurement. The extent to which this sub-objective is addressed through other means impacts the assessment of FASAB's focus on this particular sub-objective.

Internal Controls

Federal Managers' Financial Integrity Act of 1982[21] (FMFIA)--Congress has long expressed concerns about controls in various laws, dating back to the Budget and Accounting Procedures Act of 1950. The FMFIA required virtually all executive agencies to comprehensively report on internal control two decades before the Accountability for Tax Dollars Act of 2002 extended the requirement for audited financial statements to virtually all executive agencies. The requirement to report on internal controls under FMFIA and reporting on controls over financial reporting are not necessarily equivalent. Some would say that the scope of controls contemplated by FMFIA may be broader, including operational and legal compliance issues as well as financial reporting. Furthermore, judgments about materiality may be different as well.

The FMFIA requires GAO to prescribe standards of internal accounting and administrative control and agencies to comply with them. Internal control is to provide reasonable assurance that (1) obligations and costs comply with applicable law (2) assets are safeguarded against waste, loss, unauthorized use, or misappropriation, and (3) revenues and expenditures are recorded and accounted for properly so that accounts and financial and statistical reports may be prepared and the accountability of assets may be maintained.

FMFIA requires that the internal control standards include standards to ensure the prompt resolution of all audit findings. It also requires OMB to establish guidelines for agency evaluation of internal control to determine compliance with the internal control standards.

It requires agency heads to (1) annually evaluate their internal control using the OMB guidelines, and (2) annually report to the President on whether the agency's internal controls comply with the standards and objectives set forth in the FMFIA. If they do not fully comply, the report must identify the weaknesses and describe plans for correction. The report is to be signed by the head of the agency.

Impact/Analysis: SFFAC 1 includes "Systems and Control" as one of the four objectives of federal financial reporting. See discussion under OMB Circular A-123 below for a discussion of the impact/analysis of recent legislation and administrative directives.

---

[21] Although FMFIA came before the CFO Act of 1990, it is included as it is relevant for understanding how other requirements achieve the Systems and Control objective.

<u>Federal Financial Management Improvement Act of 1996 (FFMIA)</u>-- The FFMIA requires each CFO Act agency to implement and maintain financial management systems that can comply substantially with system requirements, applicable federal accounting standards, and the Standard General Ledger. For each CFO Act agency, FFMIA requires that the annual audit report state whether the agency's financial management systems comply with the requirements.

Impact/Analysis: Some may believe that the legal requirement for reporting on accounting systems' compliance with accounting standards adds a new factor for FASAB to consider. However, others may believe that compliance with law is a matter for others to assess--meaning whether an entity is in compliance with the provisions of FFMIA is a legal determination and would not affect the opinion on the financial statements. More specifically, some have argued that compliance with accounting standards (e.g., with SFFAS 4) for FFMIA may imply something different than conformance with GAAP for the purpose of expressing an opinion on financial statements. That is, some would say that an agency might be able to publish financial statements in conformance with GAAP, but not be in compliance with SFFAS 4 for purposes of FFMIA.

<u>Sarbanes-Oxley Act of 2002 (SOX)</u>--This Act contains numerous provisions affecting publicly owned companies and public accountants. Of particular interest is Section 404, "Management Assessment of Internal Controls" that requires management to assess the effectiveness of internal control and an audit attestation on the assessment made by management.

> Section 404: Management Assessment Of Internal Controls
>
> Requires each annual report of an issuer to contain an "internal control report", which shall:
>
> 1. State the responsibility of management for establishing and maintaining an adequate internal control structure and procedures for financial reporting; and
>
> 2. Contain an assessment, as of the end of the issuer's fiscal year, of the effectiveness of the internal control structure and procedures of the issuer for financial reporting.
>
> Each issuer's auditor shall attest to, and report on, the assessment made by the management of the issuer. An attestation made under this section shall be in accordance with standards for attestation engagements issued or adopted by the Board. An attestation engagement shall not be the subject of a separate engagement.

Impact/Analysis: Some have suggested that the public would expect federal practice to be comparable in this regard to what is now required of SEC registrants, and that action by FASAB to require management assertions about internal control, or at least controls over financial reporting, as an integral part of the basic financial statements would be one way to assure this. Others have suggested that existing requirements of FMFIA, FFMIA, GAGAS, and the recently revised OMB Circular A-123 (see next item for a further discussion of the impact/analysis) already accomplish a comparable result.

OMB Circular A-123 (REVISED December 2004) *Management's Responsibility for Internal Control*--In light of the new internal control requirements for publicly-traded companies (see SOX discussion above), OMB re-examined the existing internal control requirements for federal agencies. As a result, OMB Circular A-123 (which implements FMFIA) was revised to significantly strengthen the requirements for conducting management's assessment of internal control over financial reporting. The Circular is effective in fiscal year 2006.

The revised A-123 requires an assessment of internal control by management, including a separate management assurance on internal control over financial reporting. Specifically, management is required to assert to the effectiveness of internal controls via an assurance statement "as of June 30." A-123 does not require a separate audit. However, Agencies may secure a separate audit opinion on internal controls over financial reporting. In those situations, the "as of" reporting date of June 30 may be adjusted to align better with the "as of" date of the audit opinion. Also, the CFO Council and the President's Council on Integrity and Efficiency (PCIE) prepared an implementation guide to assist agencies in addressing the requirements included in A-123 Appendix A, *Internal Control over Financial Reporting*. Appendix A directs management to become more proactive in overseeing internal controls related to financial reporting.

Impact/Analysis: As noted above, SFFAC 1 includes "Systems and Control" as one of the four objectives of federal financial reporting. Based on a staff analysis of the standards issued, FASAB has not addressed this objective as much as the others in its standards. For example, it appears that SFFAS 15 may be the only standard that directly relates to the Systems and Control Objective by requiring the MD&A to address systems and controls.

Some may believe that this reference to systems and control may be sufficient and that no change is needed as a result of the strengthening of the administrative directives related to internal controls, but others may believe that an amplification of these sections of SFFAC 1 would be in order. However, other people may believe that no amplification of the concepts is needed, but that one or more statements of standards may be needed to address systems and control. Some may believe that action by FASAB to require management assertions about internal control, or at least controls over financial reporting, as an integral part of the basic financial statements would be appropriate.

Others have suggested that existing requirements of FMFIA, FFMIA, Government Audit Standards and the recently revised OMB Circular A-123 will accomplish a comparable result and has effectively ended any need for FASAB to act in this area.

<u>COMPARISON BETWEEN A-123 AND SOX</u>

	A-123	SOX
Management Assessment	Requires management assessment as of June 30[22], and update the report for any new issues coming to their attention before Sept. 30.	Requires management assessment as of the end of the company's fiscal year.
Audit Attestation	Does not require a separate audit attestation of controls over financial reporting. Note-Agencies are allowed to obtain an opinion. Also, OMB may require a separate audit if management is not achieving progress in correcting control weaknesses.	Requires audit attestation on the assessment made by management.
Framework	Provides a framework for evaluating internal controls and requires a reference to this in the management's report.	Requires management to identify the framework used to evaluate the effectiveness of controls.
Effectiveness of Controls	Precludes management from concluding internal controls are effective if there are one or more material weaknesses.	Precludes management form concluding that internal controls are effective if there are one or more material weaknesses.
Material Weaknesses	Requires management to disclose all material weaknesses as of June 30.	Requires management to disclose any material weaknesses.

<u>Department of Homeland Security Financial Accountability Act</u>--The Act requires the Department of Homeland Security management to provide an assertion on the effectiveness of internal control over financial reporting for fiscal year 2005 and requires

---

[22] Unless an audit is done, at which time the report may be dated the same as the auditors report.

an auditor's opinion on internal controls over financial reporting for fiscal years beginning after 2005. The Act also required the CFO Council and the President's Council on Integrity and Efficiency (PCIE) to study the potential costs and benefits of requiring other CFO Act agencies to obtain audit opinions on their internal control over financial reporting.

Impact/Analysis: In September 2005, the CFO Council and PCIE issued a joint report entitled *Estimating the Costs and Benefits of Opining on Agency's Internal Control over Financial Reporting.* The report concluded that given the significant incremental costs for agencies to obtain an audit opinion on internal control and the inherent differences between agencies, all CFO Act agencies should not be required to conduct such an audit at this time. Rather, agencies should be given the opportunity to continue to implement OMB Circular A-123 and obtain an internal control audit only where particular circumstances appropriately warrant such an audit.

President's Management Agenda (PMA)--*Improved Financial Performance Initiative*--As noted above, the President's Management Agenda is an aggressive strategy for improving the management of the federal government. For each initiative, there are core criteria that the agency must meet in order to get a green rating. OMB updates the scorecard on a quarterly basis.

One of the core criteria for "getting to green" on the improving financial performance initiative is: Unqualified and timely audit opinions on the annual financial statements and no material internal control weaknesses.

Impact/Analysis: OMB monitors internal control weaknesses regularly. To receive green on the PMA scorecard, agencies must eliminate all internal control weaknesses. Quarterly, OMB monitors agency performance in meeting corrective action plan targets established under the PMA scorecard. Agencies are required to submit corrective action plans to OMB to resolve internal control weaknesses reported. Quarterly, agencies are graded on their progress in achieving the corrective action milestones contained in their plans.

Conclusion on Internal Control Legislation and Administrative Directives and Linkage to Objectives

The legislation and administrative directives noted in this area focused on the improvement of agency systems of accounting, financial management, and internal controls. It appears that most of the legislation and administrative directives in this area have a direct relationship with the Systems and Control Objective. Agency efforts to comply with the legislation and administrative directives in this area (and the resulting oversight by OMB) seem to significantly contribute to meeting certain aspects of the

Systems and Control Objective. The extent to which this objective is addressed through other means impacts the assessment of FASAB's focus on this particular objective. Accordingly, GAAP standards promulgated by FASAB to meet the Systems and Control Objective do not appear to be a high priority at this time.

APPENDIX V--Objectives Roundtable Meetings

Purpose of Roundtables

The Board believed that it would be beneficial to get feedback from the community on the reporting objectives given the changes in the environment over the past 10 years. During 2005, FASAB staff conducted separate roundtable discussions on each of the four reporting objectives. The primary purpose of the discussions was to determine how the objective might be improved to facilitate its use as a means for guiding the board in developing standards of financial accounting and reporting and in developing solutions to financial accounting and reporting issues. Experts involved in specific areas, as well as those external to the accounting community provided insights on the four objectives. The roundtable meetings focused on the following general topics:

- Participant's observations on the financial reporting objective;
- Evaluating the objective in the evolutionary environment; and,
- Broad nature of the objective and determining the scope of FASAB's role.

Additionally each of the roundtable meetings focused on specific issues related to the objective being discussed.

Overall Conclusion from Roundtables

Overall, the participants agreed that the financial reporting objectives were very broad, but they did not expect FASAB or financial statement reporting to cover or meet all the objectives alone. This was consistent with the Board's view that information sources other than financial statements help to attain the objectives. The participants viewed the SFFAC 1 objectives as a broad statement of federal financial reporting objectives and not limited to objectives to be met by the development of accounting standards. The participants also expressed that FASAB should not limit itself by eliminating certain objectives in SFFAC 1. Although the participants did offer areas for improvement, there was no indication that any objective should be removed.

As for area of improvements, there were several common themes discussed in most of the Roundtable meetings that relate to enhancements of SFFAC 1 or other areas, rather than an enhancement to a particular objective. The issue areas include the following:

- Discussion of the inter-relationship of information to explain the relationship between the financial reporting objectives and the totality of reporting;
- Proactively encourage better use of the Management's Discussion and Analysis;
- Need for education and reiteration of decision usefulness as most requirements have become a compliance exercise;
- Expansion of the discussion of accountability; and,
- Better understanding of user needs--as well as internal users versus external users.

Staff believes the above items do not warrant enhancing the reporting objectives, but instead relate to possible enhancements to SFFAC 1 or other areas. However, these are prevalent issues that came up in all or most of the roundtable meetings and should be considered if the Board decides to amend SFFAC 1.

A brief summary of each of the roundtable meetings is provided below.

Budgetary Integrity Roundtable

The participants' views were consistent with the Board's views and general satisfaction with the Budgetary Integrity objective. The participants agreed that financial reporting and the related audit have improved the reliability of accounting information. Certain participants explained that although financial reports may not be useful to agency management, the fact that the reports are subjected to audit has been beneficial to improving the accuracy of the agency's underlying accounting data. Auditing the financial statements has served to improve the accounting and underlying data that the agencies use in managing programs. The participants believed that budget data has improved since agency financial reports have been subjected to audit because the audit has resulted in the identification of errors that lead to correcting budgetary reports. Additionally, the participants believed that audits help bring about consistency in definitions and improvements in controls over assets. The participants agreed that the objective was broad but FASAB or financial statement reporting was not expected to cover or meet the objective alone.

The participants also discussed issues concerning how to better achieve the objective. The topics discussed included:

- *Statement of Budgetary Resources.* Participants discussed the following concerns regarding the Statement of Budgetary Resources:

    o *Materiality and Presentation Detail.* The Statement of Budgetary Resources is prepared and audited at a very high-level. The participants explained that the materiality level is high and that it does not provide assurance that each account is accurate. Participants most actively involved in budget oversight expressed greater interest in accuracy at the account level.

- o *Conveying Accountability.* The Statement of Budgetary Resources may not demonstrate whether an entity is publicly accountable. Most participants agreed that a budget to actual comparison would provide a better report in meeting the overall Budgetary Integrity Objective. Specifically, several participants expressed the view that a budget to actual comparison at some meaningful level of detail would meet the objective of having the government publicly accountable.

- *Statement of Financing and Sub-objective 3.* Although the participants believed that the Statement of Financing was intended to achieve sub-objective 3,[23] several thought that most users do not understand the Statement of Financing and therefore, may not understand the relationship between budget and cost that it is attempting to convey. Most of the participants believed the Statement of Financing may serve as an internal document rather than a published document.

- *Internal Versus External Users.* Certain participants commented that the Board should select whether financial reporting is intended for internal or external users. It was noted that information that is important for managing an organization may not be useful for demonstrating accountability to the public at large.

- *Other Report Formats and Other Guidance Vehicles.* Participants commented that some of the PARs are lengthy and overwhelming to read. The participants agreed that it is a struggle to clearly communicate the information effectively in the PARS, but noted that many agencies are moving towards a 'popular report' or a 'condensed report' and believed that the general public may find those much more useful and interesting.

The full Summary and Analysis of the Budgetary Integrity Roundtable Meeting can be found at http://www.fasab.gov/projectsconobjectives.html as "Issue Paper for January 2006."

Operating Performance Roundtable

The participants' views regarding the Operating Performance Objective were consistent with the Board's position that the objective appears broad, but there are other

---

[23] Sub-objective 3 states, "Federal financial reporting should provide information that helps the reader to determine how information on the use of budgetary resources relates to information on the costs of programs operations and whether information on the status of budgetary resources is consistent with other accounting information on assets and liabilities."

documents and requirements that assist in accomplishing the objective. The participants confirmed that performance reporting is an important initiative in the federal government and they did not expect FASAB or financial statement reporting to cover or meet the objective alone.

The participants also discussed the following challenges to achieving the Operating Performance objective:

- *Systems and Control Issues.* Difficulty meeting fundamental requirements such as those involved in preparing financial statements for the standard financial statement audits. This condition results from existing system issues and internal control weaknesses.

- *Determining Appropriate Information to Convey and Utility of Information.* Difficulty determining the appropriate information to convey through performance measures. Additionally, the participants described that agencies are having difficulty determining unit cost information, linking that information to outcomes, and developing performance measures for some services.

- *Integrating Budget, Performance and Financial Information and Consequences.* There is a need for integration of accounting data, internal controls, financial management, and performance reporting with the capital management and performance management systems.

- *Other Report Formats and Guidance Vehicles.* Too many requirements already exist, and agencies are still trying to meet those. Any guidance issued should be less prescriptive and more open so it may be applied as needed to particular agencies. FASAB could have a role in education and providing non-authoritative guidance.

The participants discussed methods for better achieving the Operating Performance Objective as follows.

- *Cost Accounting Issues and SFFAS 4.* Participants discussed the belief that the least has been completed to achieve sub-objective 1.[24] Although some agency financial statements show the total costs of strategic goals, the notion of costs of specific programs and activities is not specifically included in the statements. FASAB could ascertain and address the conditions that are impeding the implementation of SFFAS 4.

---

[24] Sub-objective 1 states, "Federal financial reporting should provide information that helps the reader to determine the costs of providing specific programs and activities and the composition of, and changes in, these costs."

- *Sub-objective 3.* Certain participants believed that additional reporting could be done with respect to sub-objective 3.[25] Particularly, participants expressed the concern that physical assets may be underutilized in the federal government.

The complete Summary and Analysis of the Operating Performance Roundtable Meeting can be found at http://www.fasab.gov/projectsconobjectives.html as "Issue Paper for January 2006."

Stewardship Roundtable

The participants discussed the importance of the Stewardship Objective in federal financial reporting as well as their perceptions about the Stewardship Objective and FASAB's role in meeting the objective. The participants remarked that the Stewardship Objective was intended to be broad and it is currently the focus of discussions in the federal environment. The participants expressed that the Stewardship Objective is very different as it speaks to the government as a whole and the nation, and therefore is a much broader objective compared to other traditional accounting standards-setter objectives. Although most participants did believe that FASAB has an advantage in developing a reporting framework that fairly presents the financial condition of the federal government, the participants noted that much of the information needed to fulfill the Stewardship Objective is developed outside of FASAB's domain. FASAB may make a contribution by providing reporting concepts that fairly present financial condition and sustainability, accounting standards that have a complementary role in analyzing financial condition, and support for the transparency and validity of data. FASAB could say that this information is important and fits the framework that should be filled out, but the specifics of the information may be left up to others. For this and other objectives, the participants commented that a combination of accounting and other data are essential for a full assessment of whether the objective is met.

The participants also discussed various concerns and approaches for better achieving the Stewardship Objective. The discussions included the following topics:

- *Address Two Tiers of Stewardship Reporting.* Participants discussed two-tiers of financial reporting - the government broadly versus a specific program. A macro view is needed for the forward-looking long-term projections because such information could be misleading and may not make sense piecemeal. One set of criteria may be needed for reporting at the government-wide level, which would

---

[25] Sub-objective 3 states, "Federal financial reporting should provide information that helps the reader to the efficiency and effectiveness of the government's management of its assets and liabilities."

involve forward-looking projections, and perhaps another set for the component level which could discuss operating stewardship information.

- *Understanding and Reporting Financial Condition of the Nation.* The participants discussed that the Stewardship Objective concerns the government as a whole and the nation, and therefore is a much broader objective compared to other traditional accounting standards body objectives. Citizens care about information on the government and nation as a whole.

- *Projections.* Participants discussed that, given that the objective concerns how the government's and the nation's financial condition could change in the future, certain projections would be needed. However, they expressed concern that projections involve uncertainties.

- *Key National Indicators.* The participants discussed the need for economic indicators and it was noted that there appears to be a tremendous amount of interest in national indicators. The participants noted that the government has continued working on developing appropriate indicators and the information will get better with time. However, some participants were concerned because inputs are important but there may not be a cause and effect relationship.

- *Intergenerational Responsibilities.* The participants discussed that stewardship is a term with long-term implications and this should include addressing intergenerational responsibilities.

- *Other Reporting Vehicles.* Some participants commented that an approach other than traditional financial statements should be considered. A participant noted that perhaps there is a way of combining what is reported in the financial statements with what is reported in the stewardship report. The participants believed this would satisfy a need for a more comprehensive view of the financial condition of the nation.

- *Comments on the sub-objectives.* The participants believed that the objective was stated in the form of a yes/no question and could be reworded to require more of a measure of a level. Also, the participants believed that the Concepts Statement could include more narrative about why the stewardship information is needed and why it is important as this would be much more helpful than having specific examples listed in the concepts. Additional comments related to specific sub-objectives are as follows:

- ○ *Second sub-objective.*[26] Certain participants commented that the wording needs to be clarified to explain whether "sustain public services" means at a current level or future level.

- ○ *Third sub-objective.*[27] The participants expressed concern that there may not be a direct cause and effect relationship between the government operations and the nation's well-being or, if there is, it would be difficult to measure how the government is contributing.

- ▪ *Enhancing explanations throughout SFFAC 1 and Other Areas.* The participants expressed that SFFAC 1 could also be enhanced by discussing some of the knowledge that has been gained in the past 12 years. Other enhancements included the following.

  - ○ *Better Use of Management's Discussion and Analysis.* Participants believed that the thrust of better achieving the Stewardship Objective could be to better analyze existing information rather than prescribing more information. Some participants noted that perhaps the MD&A could be better utilized for communicating such information. The MD&A offers a place in the performance and accountability report to describe the interrelationship of all the information presented.

  - ○ *Determining User Needs and Decision Usefulness.* The participants noted that a differentiation between FASAB objectives and other board's objectives is meeting internal and external needs. The participants believed the notion of internal needs versus external needs could be further developed in the concepts by expanding more fully and explaining how one differentiates the two.

  - ○ *Audit Issues and Concerns.* Certain participants believed that FASAB should focus on what information needs to be presented because the issue of auditing may cloud and sometimes confuse decisions. Given that there are various levels of audit work, such as a review or agreed-upon-procedures, FASAB could first determine what information needs to be reported and next consider where it should be presented which would in turn dictate the level of audit involvement necessary.

---

[26] The second sub-objective states, "Federal financial reporting should provide information that helps the reader to determine whether future budgetary resources will likely be sufficient to sustain public services and to meet obligations as they come due."

[27] The third sub-objective states, "Federal financial reporting should provide information that helps the reader to determine whether government operations have contributed to the nation's current and future well-being."

The full Summary and Analysis of the Stewardship Roundtable Meeting can be found at http://www.fasab.gov/projectsconobjectives.html as "Issue Paper for March 2006."

Systems and Control Roundtable

The participants believed that the Systems and Control Objective remains valid in today's environment and agreed with FASAB's indirect role in achieving the objective. Most of the participants expressed support for FASAB to continue the indirect approach and did not believe that FASAB should issue a specific standard on systems and control. In addition, the participants explained that an indirect approach rather than prescriptive guidelines enables the Board to be encompassing for everyone to accomplish their mission. Some of the other comments on the objective and the role of FASAB were as follows.

- SFFAC 1 was structured to have an accountability mechanism and, given the financial challenges the nation faces, the information in the concept statement is even more important today than it was when originally crafted.

- Commercial-type audited financial statements were not viewed as the driver for affecting policy decisions at the federal level. Instead, the statements were seen as a catalyst to move individuals toward improving their accounting.

- FASAB with its limited resources should focus on addressing the direct technical accounting issues that remain and those other items on the technical agenda.

The participants also discussed ideas that could lead to better achievement of the objective. Discussions included the following:

- *Enhancing Explanations throughout SFFAC 1.* SFFAC 1 could be enhanced by discussing some of the knowledge gained since its issuance and updated to emphasize that it is not just the financial statements that enable the objectives to be met. Additional comments for enhancing SFFAC 1 are as follows:

  - *Interrelationships.* The participants indicated that there is a need to explain the relationship between the financial reporting objectives and the totality of reporting that is taking place in the federal government. It was expressed that some preparers and auditors are possibly engaging in compliance exercises or simply "checking the boxes" for many requirements, including those related to systems and control.

  - *Accountability Notion.* The participants commented that Concepts 1 was structured to have an accountability mechanism and that is why the

Concepts Statement is even more important today. They noted that Concepts 1 should be more about overall "accountability" versus "accounting."

○ *Educational Platform.* SFFAC 1 could be used as a way to convey the relationships of various reporting requirements. This may assist preparers and auditors in understanding the importance of meaningful information versus viewing it as a compliance exercise. Also, some examples of how the objectives are currently being met could be included in the discussions on each objective to help non-accountants understand the role of accountability and financial reports and the information that is used to demonstrate accountability.

○ *Other Possible Enhancements.* The participants commented on other possible enhancements to SFFAC 1 such as the statement possibly including an explanation of a financial management system; an explanation of why performance information is important; and the Concepts Statement could be updated and fine-tuned to reflect the Committee of Sponsoring Organizations of the Treadway Commission (COSO) changes and perhaps the changes that COSO is now considering.

The full Summary and Analysis of the Systems and Control Roundtable Meeting can be found at http://www.fasab.gov/projectsconobjectives.html as "Issue Paper for March 2006."

FASAB Board Members

David Mosso, Chairman

Tom L. Allen
Claire Gorham Cohen
Robert F. Dacey
John A. Farrell
Donald B. Marron
James M. Patton
Robert N. Reid
Alan H. Schumacher
Danny Werfel

FASAB Staff

Wendy M. Comes, Executive Director

Melissa L. Loughan
Ross E. Simms

Federal Accounting Standards Advisory Board
441 G Street NW, Suite 6814
Mail Stop 6K17V
Washington, DC 20548
Telephone 202-512-7359
FAX 202-512-7366
www.fasab.gov

---

www.ingramcontent.com/pod-product-compliance
Lightning Source LLC
Chambersburg PA
CBHW052009280526
45793CB00005B/903